THE NEW NASHVILLE CHEF'S TABLE

THE NEW NASHVILLE CHEF'S TABLE

EXTRAORDINARY RECIPES FROM MUSIC CITY

STEPHANIE STEWART-HOWARD

WITH PHOTOGRAPHY BY RON MANVILLE

Globe
Pequot

Guilford, Connecticut

This book is dedicated to my husband Seth Howard,
for all the love and support he's given to me,
and to my late grandmothers, Myra Stewart and Lula Webb,
who introduced me to the art of Southern food.
For the second edition, I add my parents, Joe and Yvonne Stewart,
because without their constant culinary challenges,
I'd never be the cook I am today.

Globe Pequot

An imprint of The Rowman & Littlefield Publishing Group, Inc.
4501 Forbes Blvd., Ste. 200
Lanham, MD 20706
www.rowman.com

Distributed by NATIONAL BOOK NETWORK

British Library Cataloguing in Publication Information Available

Library of Congress Cataloging-in-Publication Data Available

ISBN 978-1-4930-3418-5 (hardcover)
ISBN 978-1-4930-3419-2 (e-book)

♾™ The paper used in this publication meets the minimum requirements of American National Standard for Information Sciences—Permanence of Paper for Printed Library Materials, ANSI/NISO Z39.48-1992.

Printed in the United States of America

Restaurants and chefs often come and go, and menus are ever-changing. We recommend you call ahead to obtain current information before visiting any of the establishments in this book.

CONTENTS

acknowledgments

Trying to represent Nashville's burgeoning food culture in such a small space has been a stunning task. I owe a lot of gratitude to the people who taught me what food and food writing are all about in this spectacular town.

The marvelous Martha Stamps familiarized me in so many ways with Nashville's traditional food culture, and food critic Kay West introduced me to both the newest and the oldest of the restaurants that define who we are as a culinary city. Miss Daisy King reminds me what Nashville cooking is truly all about with everything she does.

My friends and fellow writers Chris Chamberlain, Jennifer Justus, Dara Carson, Melissa Corbin, Natasha Lorens, Nicki Pendleton Wood, Vivek Surti, and Tammy Algood have inspired me, as have the chefs and artists who have become more than passing acquaintances, including Pat Martin, Tyler Brown, Jason McConnell, Carl Schultheis, Tandy Wilson, Siva Pavuluri, Sarah Souther, James Hensley, Maneet Chauhan, and Sarah Scarborough. Marne Duke, Robin Riddell Jones, Janet Kurtz, Martha Stamps, and Jennifer Hagan-Dier, thanks for your knowledge and advice over the years. Dr. Van West and Nelson Eddy, thank you for the Rutherford culinary scene endorsements. Vincent Farone, Jenny Newell, Sean and Jaimi Reisz, Carol Kirk, Micaela Burnham, Abby Stranathan, Amy Ripton—thank you for foodie inspiration every time you cook. Lara Olstad, the cocktails were much appreciated—Peeptinis forever. Bart and Megan Roegner, thanks for being our dining buddies. Brandi Fleck, Shannon McCue, Mike Donley, Chad Evans, and Brian Peters: thank you all for making my day job environment awesome while I was rewriting this book at night. Additional thanks to Krishna Adams for aid in collecting arts information. A big thank you to my sister, Laura Holder, at the MTSU Gore Center for Historic Preservation, for helping me with the historic tourism materials I added to this edition of the book.

My parents, Joe and Yvonne Stewart, opened up the culinary world for me, not only from their own Southern background, but through world travel and the opportunity to experience native foods across the globe—and they taught me to bring the recipes home and cook them for myself. They are both outstanding cooks, and I'm lucky they still believe in family meals.

Likewise, my late grandmothers, Myra Fendley Stewart and Lula Prillaman Webb, were my first teachers about eating fresh food you grew yourself and just how good the simplest things, like biscuits and yeast rolls, could be. (Needless to say, they were also both absolute masters of the complex, especially when it came to dessert.)

The greatest thanks of all belong to my husband, Seth Howard, who encouraged me to pursue my dreams and put up with my incessant talk about this book. He is my constant source of inspiration in all the arts I pursue and the goals I make for myself.

INTRODUCTION

I never expected to write a second edition of this book. I can't imagine being happier that I did. Middle Tennessee expands more every day. It is bursting with not only starry-eyed musicians and singers, but also tech entrepreneurs, chefs, and artists of myriad varieties—people from all over the country drawn to the magic and innovation that is Nashville. Every time you expect it to slow and trickle out, it surprises you—finding new and inventive ways to draw tourists and new residents. I am thrilled to witness the changes this city makes every few weeks. It is a bright beacon of the best parts of the South. I suspect we still have a long way to go to define ourselves in the eyes of the world at large, but it's a grand journey. Hype lasts for a moment, but behind hype is innovation that will keep things percolating here for decades.

Nashville has been a music town for decades now, ever since the Grand Ole Opry began in the 1930s with the rise of "old-time" music, followed by an even greater musical influx after World War II, with the birth of Music Row. It dates back to the days of RCA Studio B, on to Hank and Patsy, through George and Tammy and Dolly and Porter, then Willie and Kris and Johnny and Merle, on to Garth Brooks and George Strait, to Carrie Underwood and Blake Shelton. We've been viewed through the eyes of *Hee Haw* and Robert Altman's *Nashville* and *Nashville* the TV show. But there is more to "Music City" than years of music—then and now.

Two thousand thirteen, the year the first edition of this book was written, saw Nashville become an "it" city in the eyes of the nation and the world—about, for once, more than just the musical superstars. Dozens of publications, domestic and international, rushed to talk about us—our food, our arts, our craftspersons, our businesses, our sports, and our real estate—and proclaim us the hottest thing in the nation.

Well, that's nice and all, but most of those things were here prior to now, and more will happen when the fickle media has moved on to Cleveland, Syracuse, or Billings—as it has in some ways already. The eyes of the world will still be on us, because we genuinely have that much to offer, even if we aren't the "hot new thing." We are our own thing, thriving and strong.

In this moment, as the world rediscovers us, our culinary culture is blooming. Unlike Charleston and New Orleans, we don't have a fundamentally defined cuisine that's spent two hundred years fermenting into something distinct. We have instead a food history that is deeply tied to the history of the South itself.

Nashville, and the areas surrounding it in Davidson, Williamson, and Rutherford Counties, had a thriving Native American culture for centuries before European settlers arrived. In 1779 James Robertson and John Donelson left North Carolina and set up Fort Nashborough, a replica of which can still be visited today. The presence of the Cumberland and Harpeth Rivers provided myriad advantages, from irrigation for cotton fields to river transport, and a city was born.

The nineteenth century offered up notable pieces of American history, from presidents Andrew Jackson, James K. Polk, and Andrew Johnson to Civil War battles

and occupation. Not all of it was good and pretty—Tennessee was one of the states with supporters of both sides of the Civil War, and we still carry those scars. After the Civil War, Nashville grew up as a center of trade, thanks to the railroads. If it had any national culinary claim to fame prior to World War II, it was probably the celebrated coffee blend at the Maxwell House Hotel downtown.

As one of my local culinary heroines, Miss Daisy King, tells it, until comparatively recently there was no defined restaurant history in Nashville. What you got when you visited the city were a lot of chain-type places, with a few notable local spots—many more renowned for the songwriters who hung out there than for the food served. All the big department stores, such as downtown's late, lamented Cain-Sloan, had their own in-house restaurants, and a few places, such as Sperry's and Jimmy Kelly's (both steak houses), managed to make names for themselves as fine-dining institutions by the 1970s (Kelly's dates to 1934).

Miss Daisy's own famous tearoom got its start in Franklin (just to the south of Nashville proper) in 1974 and helped define the moment's "taste" of Nashville. During the 1980s locally owned places finally started to gain a slender foothold, though most were downtown or in Green Hills, not spread out in the smaller neighborhoods—unless you counted small iconic places like Bobby's Dairy Dip in Sylvan Park.

When my parents moved here some twenty years ago the chains still dominated. A handful of really good locally owned places had sprung up by then—F. Scott's, Jay Pennington's Bound'ry, and Randy Rayburn's Sunset Grill among them—and the owners of these and other locations banded together to form Nashville Originals, an organization to promote and support independent restaurant owners in and around the city. That organization still thrives today, though those restaurants are gone, supporting Nashville Restaurant Week and providing deals to patrons who come out and explore locally owned eateries.

I jumped in and out of the city until about 2004, when I settled here permanently and reinvented myself from grad student and theater professional to journalist. Over the past years, the restaurant scene has changed uncannily fast. Talented chefs, many trained under culinary experts at our own longer-standing originals, are branching out and starting their own places, and new chefs are moving to town to start their careers here, rather than choosing larger, more trafficked locations.

Neighborhood restaurants are cropping up—not with the aim of being giant powerhouses, but intending to serve very good food of all types to people who live nearby and help build neighborhood cultures. Germantown, Sylvan Park, East Nashville, and even longtime holdout and chain-centric Franklin are now thriving with those new establishments—places that, in the words of local supper club creator and chef Avon Lyons, "are manageable, with delicious food. They're focused on sharing with just enough people, not trying to bring in massive crowds and not spending the budget on public relations."

We find these restaurants everywhere now, from the older and more established, such as East Nashville's Margot Cafe, to Jason McConnell's more recent Red Pony in Franklin or Germantown's brand-new Rolf and Daughters. Even the exceptional "old-school" spots, such as Capitol Grille in the Hermitage Hotel, attain that feel, thanks to the work of their chefs and dedicated staffs. We tend to favor intimacy over the overblown and outsized.

With our growing interest in fresh foods and the spread of the Slow Food movement and other concepts like it, we've built an exceptional system of farmers' markets, with one accessible to nearly everyone, regardless of where you live in the city, and a huge and thriving downtown Nashville Farmers' Market. These markets not only help us support local farms and make fresh produce more readily available, but also encourage and support up-and-coming chefs, restaurateurs, and artisan food producers.

Nashville has moved from a place where a few restaurants had microbrew options to thriving microbreweries all over the city—Yazoo, Jackalope, Blackstone, Mantra, Mayday (in nearby Murfreesboro), Fat Bottom, Cool Springs, Corsair, and more—some of which are gaining serious national attention. A change in our state laws has made Tennessee's microdistilleries, many centered in and around the Nashville area (Pennington's, Corsair Artisan, Nelson's Greenbrier, and H. Clark), something to be talked about on a worldwide level. And each May the Toast to Tennessee Wine Festival comes to town, showcasing the state's thirty-some wineries and underlining that places such as Château Ross, Beachhaven, and Arrington Vineyards are making things that aren't the syrupy wine equivalent of overly sweet tea.

In the past few years, we've evolved further still: Scott Witherow's Olive & Sinclair chocolate company and Sarah Scarborough's Firepot Nomadic Teas make a good representation of the plethora of small, artisan food businesses that have emerged, impacted our food landscape, and moved to national prominence.

Amidst all this growth, our chefs have become the backbone of the rising trend of the farm-to-fork movement that's still growing forty years after Alice Waters popularized the idea. More, they're reintroducing us to the things that are best about Southern food. What was once intrinsic to the Nashville and Southeastern diet is being rediscovered.

So what is Tennessee food, anyway? Like most of the cuisine native to the South, it depends on

seasonal eating and what's available on the farm at the time. It is the food of farmers more than it is the culinary creation of the affluent, and like much of what we love best about classic French or Italian country cuisine, it grows out of a need to make the best possible with what one has at hand. It's food that evolved through the era of slavery and Jim Crow, that we never entirely felt comfortable admitting we owed to innovative African-American cooks whose names are now lost to history, something we still struggle to come to terms with, even as we acknowledge that "Southern" food has myriad parallels with Soul food. Tennessee food is not exclusive to one race's experience, and that is important to understand.

At its heart, traditional Southern food is tied to the food all our grandparents ate growing up during the Depression, which isn't all that different from what their own parents and grandparents ate during their farm-based childhoods. Many of us who are adults now are fortunate enough to have had grandparents and great-grandparents who still maintained "gardens" (my grandparents essentially had small farms in town)

through our childhoods, who canned the fresh produce or froze it and sent it home in boxes with us each time we visited.

What you got was straightforward: corn and beans, peppers, greens, squashes, and pumpkins; tomatoes whole and made into sauces; chow chows and pickles, and even old-style fermented sauerkrauts. Jellies and jams and preserves were there, too, made from the fruit they or the neighbors grew. Today we connect all of that with the notion of farm-to-fork and somehow often forget that it's a rediscovery, not a new thing.

Coming from a Southern family (Virginia and South Carolina, in full disclosure), albeit one centered first in the military, then corporate America, I learned about this kind of food from my own parents and grandparents. The first thing I learned to cook was biscuits, by the time I was about six years old. Self-rising flour, shortening, milk—even a kid could do it, and knead dough, and make a good biscuit. To this day I can make them without ever resorting to a measuring cup and still get it right. Thanks, Mom.

My friends are learning how to can again, and make jams and preserves. Dara Carson, who has a farm of her own as well as a little house "in town," is my constant inspiration in this. We're learning to forage—flowers like honeysuckle for simple syrups, wild berries and herbs, morels. In part we're learning it because it's on trend, no doubt about that. But in a few years it may not be, and we will still have the skill. We've learned to appreciate the taste of things that don't come from supermarket shelves—that are fresh, or freshly preserved—and value that which we make with our own hands.

Many of us are buying chicken, pork, or beef directly from the farmers. There is new appreciation for game meats like wild turkey, duck, and venison, and freshly caught fish that we can fry up in cornmeal or grill. Barbecue is a thing for us—slow-cooking meats until they are tender to falling apart, then shredding them with a good fork.

And with that, as we follow the trends, we've returned to the Southern foodways of previous generations. Into it we've blended the popular post–World War II starches, like macaroni and cheese, and made them our own with willful delight.

When we prepare these simple, fresh foods, cooking them in a traditional manner—the turnip greens long simmered with a bit of pork, the tomatoes and cucumbers marinated overnight in vinegar and oil—we return to our roots.

Nashville's chef contingent is very aware of this past, and true to it. A few of them, most notably Tyler Brown and Matt Lackey, have turned farmer themselves. That doesn't mean that they aren't also blending in the tastes and traditions of other cultures—hints of South Asia and France, Germany and Morocco. They are indeed. And the arrival of Food Network

star and international chef extraordinaire Maneet Chauhan has inspired a new level of introspection and invention—the blending of traditional foods of many cultures into a rich hybrid that may be the new normal of American eating. I hope dearly that it's the wave of the future, and that this kind of fusion builds, continues, and makes us richer for it.

In point of fact, we have grown to enjoy ethnic food as a city in a way we never have before. But what seems to underlie the best of all of it now is the understanding that the shared past of fresh food and seasonal flavors—in our Southern culture and in others—produces the best meals. And it is the root of all our flavorful cooking.

When putting together this cookbook, I was faced with the daunting task of sorting out the most representative of Nashville's restaurant scene. My preliminary list had over a hundred places on it, and I've reduced it to half that for you here. I hope it will serve not only as a cookbook, but also as a guide to all Nashville has to offer, whether you're cooking for your family or planning a trip to the area.

As I wrote this book, chefs I knew well were making announcements about new places and spaces across the city. In the three and a half years since, it's become almost impossible to trace all their tracks without an app for that—exploring new ideas and mapping new culinary ground. I can only imagine that things will grow more exciting and expansive in the coming years, whether we are an "it" city of the moment or not.

ARNOLD'S COUNTRY KITCHEN

605 8th Avenue South, The Gulch
(615) 256-4455
arnoldscountrykitchen.com

The mythic meat and three restaurant that dominates the Southern landscape gets taken to the next level with Arnold's Country Kitchen. It's not just the James Beard Foundation America's Classic Award or Guy Fieri's *Diners, Drive-Ins and Dives* that make that definitive, but the locals who line up daily from the moment the doors unlock. Set just at the boundary of The Gulch on 8th Avenue South, Arnold's has been a legend since Jack Arnold and his wife, Rose, started the whole thing thirty years ago. The chef these days is Jack's gifted son Kahlil, who astounds me both with his graciousness and his talent every time I walk in the place.

You never know just exactly what will turn up on the menu, though a board advertises the entrees by day of the week. The tiny space is always filled for lunch (no dinners, sorry), and you should expect to share a table if you and your party don't fill it up (there are plenty of two-tops).

When I go in, I have to admit a weakness for the roast beef, which Arnold's legends are made of, but there's also the fried chicken, the pork, the meat loaf—oh, man, the meat loaf. But meat and three culture prides itself on doing traditional Southern foods right, and the catfish served up by Kahlil Arnold and his folks is meant to be enjoyed. If you're not catching them yourself, your grocery store or fishmonger should have them, even if you live in a non-catfish-centric part of the nation.

CATFISH

(SERVES 4–6)

5–6 (5–7 ounces each) farm-raised catfish fillets

8 cups warm water

3 tablespoons kosher salt

3 tablespoons hot sauce
(Louisiana Hot Sauce preferred)

3 cups enriched, self-rising white cornmeal
(White Lily preferred)

2 teaspoons salt

2 teaspoons black pepper

2 teaspoons granulated garlic

1 teaspoon cayenne pepper

6–8 cups canola oil

To brine the catfish, fill a bowl with warm water (hot tap water is fine) and whisk in kosher salt and hot sauce until salt dissolves. Put mixture in the freezer for 15–20 minutes. Remove from freezer and put catfish fillets in brine. (I usually put some ice cubes on top to keep the fish really cold.) Put in the fridge for about 3 hours or overnight.

When the fish is ready to be fried, mix the cornmeal, salt, pepper, garlic, and cayenne pepper in a bowl.

Remove catfish from fridge. Drain and rinse off brine with cold water in a colander. Let excess water drain completely off.

Heat canola oil in a deep-dish sauté pan or iron skillet, making sure you don't put too much oil in

it. You want to fill it a little less than halfway. Check the temperature with an oil thermometer. When the oil gets to 335°F, it's ready to go and you can turn it down a little.

Dredge both sides of the catfish in the cornmeal mixture. Shake off excess meal. Place the catfish in the skillet and cook for 5–6 minutes. Turn catfish over halfway with metal tongs during cooking if needed to get both sides browned.

Remove fish and set on a plate lined with paper towels so excess oil can drain. After about 15 seconds, it's ready to serve.

THE THREES

Khalil Arnold's Southern Green Beans, Mac & Cheese, and Tomato Basil Pie all complement the catfish recipe above. There are plenty of entrees you can pair them with, of course, but the trio together is fairly marvelous—hence the "meat and three" concept. And all of them meet the "kid food" challenge when you're cooking for family.

These days, after a shift away from fresh foods over the past few decades, local produce, fresh and grown nearby, is making a comeback. Kahlil's mom, Rose, once told me that much of hers came from early-morning visits to the Nashville Farmers' Market. Once you taste their food, it's easy to believe the Arnolds don't take fresh for granted.

The whole advantage to the meat and three style is that you get to choose from a wide variety to make up your plate.

SOUTHERN GREEN BEANS
(SERVES 8–10)

4 slices applewood smoked bacon, chopped

1 medium onion, chopped

1 tablespoon canola oil

2 pounds fresh-cut green beans

Pinch of crushed red pepper

6–8 cups chicken broth

Salt and freshly ground black pepper to taste

In a medium-size pot on medium-high heat, sauté the bacon for 5 minutes, stirring with a wooden spoon until browned.

Add onions and canola oil and stir for 3 minutes, until onions start looking translucent.

Add green beans, red pepper, and chicken broth and cook on same heat until half of the broth has evaporated, stirring every few minutes. It should take around 30 minutes. The longer you cook, the more flavor the green beans will absorb. Add water if needed.

Reduce heat to low and taste. Add salt and pepper if needed.

MAC & CHEESE

(SERVES 6–8)

Ask anyone what their favorite comfort food is, and if mac and cheese isn't on the list, they're probably lying. There are several variations on the genre in this book, but this one is fairly easy and really delicious.

8 cups water

2 tablespoons canola oil

2 cups macaroni noodles

2 tablespoons margarine

2 tablespoons flour

2 cups milk

2½ cups shredded American cheese, divided

1 teaspoon black pepper

1 teaspoon ground mustard seed

2 tablespoons grated Parmesan cheese

Pinch of salt

Paprika

In a medium pot, bring water to a boil. Add canola oil and noodles. Cook for 20 minutes, or until noodles swell and are soft. Drain in a colander.

Meanwhile, preheat oven to 325°F.

In a double boiler, melt margarine. When melted, stir in flour and cook for a few minutes until browned. Slowly add milk, whisking vigorously.

Add 2 cups of shredded cheese and stir until melted. Whisk in black pepper, mustard, and Parmesan cheese. Taste to see if a pinch of salt is needed.

In a small casserole dish, add noodles and stir in cheese sauce. Sprinkle remaining ½ cup of shredded cheese on top. Lightly sprinkle paprika on top.

Put in preheated oven and cook for 30 minutes, or until cheese is bubbling around edges.

TOMATO BASIL PIE

(SERVES 6–8)

Tomato Basil Pie also touches on the Southern love for dairy products, even though the artisan cheese movement is a new thing for us. Both mac and cheese and this pie manage to make it to the top of the comfort food list, with their insistence on creamy cheeses.

4 medium fresh local tomatoes

1 9-inch frozen pie shell

3 tablespoons Cavender's All Purpose Greek Seasoning or to taste (available in most grocery store spice and seasoning aisles or from lacrawfish.com)

1 cup fresh basil, chopped

¾ cup mayonnaise

3 cups shredded mild cheddar cheese

First, wash and core the tomatoes. Thinly slice the tomatoes and put on a plate lined with paper towels. You should have at least 3 layers and make sure there are paper towels between each layer. Refrigerate for at least 3 hours to let some of the juice from the tomatoes drain so the pie is not soggy.

Prebake pie shell for 30 minutes at 325°F. To keep the bottom from puffing, you should line the bottom crust with parchment paper and fill it with dried

beans. After prebaking the crust and letting it cool, remove the beans and parchment paper.

Next, remove the tomatoes from the fridge. Cover the bottom of the piecrust with a layer of tomatoes. Shake the Cavender's on the layer of tomatoes and sprinkle some basil on them. Repeat the process for the next two layers.

In a separate mixing bowl, mix the mayo and cheese into a paste with a spatula. Put the cheese mixture on the top of the pie, smoothing it out with the spatula. Bake for 30–45 minutes or until it starts to turn golden brown.

THE MEAT AND THREE

I'm not sure anyone can define the moment when the meat and three concept came into being, though it's probably a century or better back in time. What I am sure of is that you find it throughout the South, from Virginia to Louisiana, in various formats.

In Tennessee they're on every corner, some in nicer buildings, others in cinderblock shacks or gas stations along the rural routes you drive between Nashville and McMinnville or Sparta. The building is no indication of how good the food is—some of the best food is in some of the most rickety and rundown spaces.

Corporate-culture chains now take the meat and three concept to the masses, but things change as they attempt to appeal to everyone—there's no raspberry iced tea or jalapeño popper starter brought to your table at a true meat and three. Real ones generally involve a cafeteria-style line: Choose your meat—fried chicken, roast beef with gravy, pork barbecue, chicken livers, catfish, and so on—and pair it with sides. Note I don't say "vegetables," because while you find cucumbers and tomatoes, greens, beans, succotash, and such, there's plenty of starch—mashed potatoes, corn bread, macaroni and cheese, grits—and deep-fried options such as cornmeal-crusted okra.

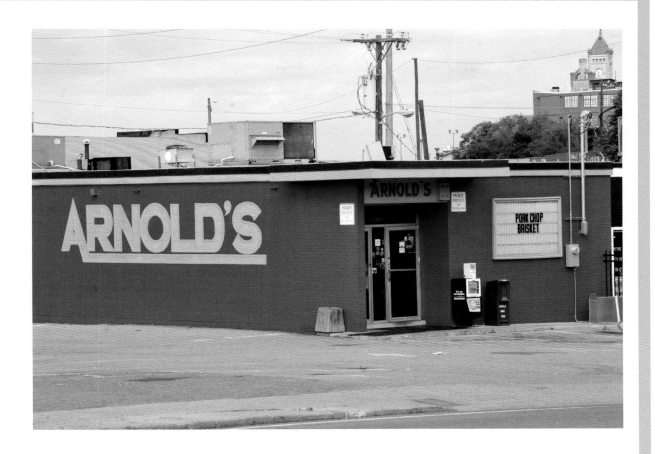

In Nashville, folks like the Arnold family of Arnold's Country Kitchen have turned true meat and three into an art form. Others have modernized the traditional Southern foodways, adapting favorite recipes into fine-dining variations.

You'll find any number of classic meat and three recipes in this book—some in old-school formats, some taken in new directions. There are four takes on mac and cheese, for example, from the adult wonder of Cabana's, made as a grown-up main course with lobster and brie, and Whiskey Kitchen's spicy Southwest-influenced chipotle variation, to Arnold's straightforward meat and three style, perfect for pairing with the catfish recipe they've provided.

Together they underline how the South's foodways evolve to meet the needs of contemporary diners.

THE BANG CANDY COMPANY

1300 Clinton Street, Suite 127, Germantown/North Nashville
(615) 953-1065
bangcandycompany.com

I first met Sarah Souther a few years ago, when she was a regular at events at the Nashville Farmers' Market with her Coco-Van, serving hot cocoa and homemade marshmallows of devastating goodness during the cold months. Then, during my days at a city magazine, I had interns Ali and Olivia, who wanted to be food writers. To celebrate the end of the semester, they brought me a box of artisan rosewater-scented, chocolate-dipped marshmallows from the kitchen of Sarah Souther. I was hooked.

Today, Sarah has turned her business into a brick-and-mortar, leaving long lines outside the Bang Candy Company shop at Marathon Motor Works in Germantown, some waiting for a refreshing lunch of soups, salads, and sandwiches, others clamoring for her homemade confections.

I have a real weakness for her "boozy" salted caramels these days. Even more, her magical simple syrups are now de rigueur on friends' bars, for mixing cocktails. The Sarah special is a glass of Prosecco with one of them added in. I favor the Rosemary Ginger, which has a marvelous ginger beer pop in a little bubbly.

I'm thrilled Sarah's given me a complex confection for the book. "This little delight marries myriad tastes and sensations, it is absolutely irresistible," she says. "There are a few steps but don't be put off—it will be worth it in the end!" She's right.

"You will need a mixer, a thermometer, a forcing bag and tip, and a blowtorch amongst the usual kitchen bits and bobs," per Sarah.

RASPBERRY LEMON CLOUD 9

(MAKES 30 SMALL COOKIES)

For the cookies:

3 sticks (1½ cups) unsalted butter, room temperature

1 cup sugar

1 large egg

½ teaspoon fine sea salt

1 teaspoon vanilla extract

3¼ cups all-purpose flour

Fine sugar, for rolling

¾ cup raspberry jam (Sarah prefers seedless when piping the jam because seeds can catch in the bag.)

For the marshmallow ("cloud"):

3 teaspoons gelatin

⅓ cup plus ¼ cup water, divided

1 cup sugar

¼ teaspoon salt

Zest of 1 lemon

½ teaspoon vanilla

To make the cookies: Preheat oven to 350°F.

Beat butter and sugar in mixer until light and fluffy. Add egg, salt, and vanilla and beat until completely combined. With mixer on low, add flour and mix just until incorporated.

Shape dough into 1-inch balls and roll them in fine sugar. Place on baking sheets, at least 3 inches apart. Squish slightly with the bottom of a glass, then make an imprint with your thumb.

Bake for 10 minutes, then remove from the oven and fill imprint with raspberry jam. Place back in the oven for another 10 minutes, then remove and let cool.

To make the marshmallow ("cloud"): Bloom the gelatin in ⅓ cup water in the bottom of the mixer. On the stove, heat sugar and ¼ cup water to 240°F (use a digital thermometer).

Pour syrup into mixer bowl while running at low speed. Once incorporated, add salt and increase speed gradually up to high. The marshmallow will become glossy and opaque, similar to meringue. Add lemon zest and vanilla. (You must be *very* attentive. There is a sweet spot you are trying to achieve with the marshmallow—too runny and you'll have a mess on your hands; too stiff and you won't be able to pipe it properly.)

Keep whipping. When you think it's nearly there, stop mixer and lift whisk. The stream of mallow should keep its shape and flow fairly easily. ("Don't worry, it may take several tries, but like riding a bicycle, you'll only have to learn once," says Sarah. "And the end result is so worth it.")

To assemble: When it's time, you have to move quickly to prevent the marshmallow from congealing in the bag. With speed, transfer mallow into forcing bag and pipe onto the cooled cookies.

Let cool, then roll in fine sugar (this prevents them from sticking together). When ready to serve, hit them with the kitchen torch and lightly toast the marshmallow.

Result: A crunchy, sweet, tart, gooey, warm, high-speed elevator to Cloud 9.

Barlines

Omni Nashville Hotel
250 5th Avenue South, Nashville
(615) 782-5300
omnihotels.com/hotels/nashville/dining/barlines

So, at some point most of us have had a cocktail or two in Barlines, if we live here in Nashville. My first venture involved drinking whisky with James Hensley (formerly of Patterson House, now at Nelson's Greenbrier) after we'd done a panel discussion at a conference on local distilleries and our foodie friend Chris Chamberlain (I have vague memories of Vivek Surti being part of this too). We plotted starting an insane foodie podcast with some other writers, which never quite came about, but I still remember having an outstanding Manhattan. Be aware, in the evening, Barlines is twenty-one and over only. The bar is a major selling point.

Barlines, with live music and plenty of atmosphere, is my own favorite destination of the Omni's three restaurants, though all have excellent points to draw you in. When no one is playing, the abundant TVs offer up our favorite sports teams—and this is a sports-loving town.

The menu highlights original takes on bar standards, including killer burgers, appetizers, and grown up milkshakes for the crowd with the necessary IDs. They offer an absolutely delish smoked brisket grilled cheese, and were thoughtful enough to tell us how that make that brisket, so we can add it to our own sandwiches at home.

SMOKED BRISKET

(SERVES 20+)

Whole brisket comes in an average size of 15–16 pounds. Reduce the ingredient percentages as needed, based on the size you're using.

Whole brisket, trim ¼ inch fat, aged 30 days, choice or higher grade prime is preferred

½ cup Kosher salt (½ teaspoon per pound of meat, assuming 15–16 pounds of brisket—reduce as needed)

3 tablespoons coarsely ground black pepper

1 tablespoon white granulated sugar

1 tablespoon onion powder

2 teaspoons mustard powder

2 teaspoons garlic powder

2 teaspoons New Mexico red chili powder or ancho chili powder

1 teaspoon ground cayenne or chipotle pepper

Enough water as needed to make a paste

Apple juice as needed to spray smoking brisket

Trim meat, leaving ¼ inch fat around brisket.

Combine salt and all spices, mix with water, and rub entire brisket with the rub; let sit on rack and dry uncovered in fridge overnight up to 24 hours.

Pre-heat smoker to 225°F. Change wood every two hours if needed.

Place brisket, fat side down, on racks; spray with apple juice every two hours. Smoke until brisket reaches 155°F internal temperature with probe thermometer. This can take 3–5 hours.

Remove from smoker, spray with more apple juice, double wrap extremely tight with foil. Place back in smoker. Cook until it reaches an internal temperature of 200°F; this can take an additional 2–4 hours depending on size of the brisket.

Remove from smoker and place in insulated container wrapped and insulated with paper or towels. Wrap tight and let sit for up to 3 hours. Remove from container.

Let it rest before you carve. If unwrapped, it should come down to an internal temp of 140°F. Chop or slice warm.

Serve immediately with favorite bun, coleslaw and barbecue sauce on the side.

BASTION

434 Houston Street, Nashville
(615) 490-8434
bastionnashville.com

Set in the burgeoning Houston-Wedgewood neighborhood, Bastion has both a bar and kitchen aspect. If you're in the bar, it's all about craft cocktails and microbrews. The only food offerings on that side are incredible nachos, with a pungent black hot sauce—and we have the recipe here. On the kitchen side a tiny, cozy neighborhood restaurant seats up to twenty-four guests (no parties more than six, please) for an ever changing, five-course a la carte menu.

Bastion, like so many other original concepts in the city, comes to us as a brainchild of Strategic Hospitality. When the Goldberg brothers started, quirky, innovated concepts were still something of a pipedream in Nashville. Now, they have challenged other food and drink entrepreneurs to raise the bar and alter the status quo—something for which we are extremely grateful.

BASTION NACHOS

(SERVES 6-8)

12–16 ounces tortilla chips (1 large bag)

1 3- to 4-pound smoked or rotisserie chicken, shredded (about 2 cups of meat)

1 cup grated American cheese

1 cup Bastion Queso, warm (recipe follows)

½ cup pickled jalapeño slices

½ cup pickled red onions

½ cup sliced black olives

2 radishes, thinly sliced

½ cup cilantro, chopped

½ cup sour cream

½ cup crumbled Cotija cheese

1 cup Raw Tomatillo Salsa (recipe follows)

Black Hot Sauce, for serving (recipe follows)

Preheat the oven to 400°F. Arrange half of the chips on a rimmed baking sheet. Scatter half of the chicken and American cheese over the chips. Repeat to form a second layer of chips, chicken and cheese. Bake until the cheese has melted, about 5–7 minutes.

Pour a generous amount of queso over the chips. Arrange the remaining toppings over the chips and serve with tomatillo salsa and hot sauce on the side and/or drizzled over the chips.

BASTION QUESO

(MAKES 2 CUPS)

1 cup whole milk

1 cup beer (nothing hoppy)

2 tablespoons pickled jalapeño brine

1 pound Velveeta Queso Blanco, shredded

In a large saucepan, combine the milk, beer, and jalapeño brine. Bring to a simmer over medium-high heat, then whisk in the Velveeta until it's melted and glossy. Keep warm until ready to use.

RAW TOMATILLO SALSA

(MAKES ABOUT 2 CUPS)

1 pound tomatillos (about 6 medium)—husks removed, washed and quartered

½ small white onion, diced

1 large jalapeño pepper (with or without seeds), coarsely chopped

1 large garlic clove, chopped

1 tablespoon Kosher salt

2 teaspoons sugar

In a blender, combine the tomatillos, onion, jalapeño and garlic. Stir in the salt and sugar and refrigerate until ready to use, up to 3 days.

BLACK HOT SAUCE

(MAKES 1½ CUPS)

1 small white onion, cut into ½-inch slices

1 large poblano pepper

3 jalapeño peppers

3 serrano peppers

3 habanero peppers

1 bulb roasted garlic, separated into cloves

1 tablespoon honey

Kosher salt, to taste

Prepare a hot grill or preheat the broiler to high. Grill (or broil) the onions and peppers, turning frequently, until blackened all over, removing the smaller peppers as they're finished (the poblanos will take the longest). When the peppers are cool enough to handle, discard the stems and seeds (or leave the seeds in if you like a very spicy salsa). Transfer the peppers to a blender, add the garlic and honey and blend at high speed until the sauce is smooth; season to taste with salt. Refrigerate until ready to use (up to 1 week).

BELLA NASHVILLE

900 Rosa L. Parks Boulevard (Nashville Farmers' Market), Germantown
(615) 457-3863
bellanashville.com

Nashville is getting a reputation as a pizza town, although it seems like many of the new pizza places opening right now are either chains or extensions of high-end pizza places from outside the area. Happily, Bella Nashville is all our own.

The arrival of Bella Nashville in 2012 is one of the post–flood of 2010 changes that helped really revitalize the Nashville Farmers' Market. Set in the southeast corner of the market shed, there's always a crowd clamoring for their handmade personal pizza, and the atmosphere is redolent with the odors of Tuscany and Florence.

On my very first visit, not long after they opened, I spoke with co-owner Emma Berkey as I tried to decide my order. After hearing that my migraines limited my dairy intake, she wisely advised me to substitute a little truffle oil in place of the cheese on my pizza—and totally won my heart. It was delicious. I took a cheesy variant home to my husband, and we've been hooked ever since.

Part of what makes Bella Nashville special is not only the creative use of ingredients, but also the pizza oven made of French white clay. This isn't fooling around with perfection; it's making the perfect even more sublime.

This recipe focuses on two of my very favorite things: Brussels sprouts and bacon. (You can get Tennessee's legendary Benton's Bacon and ham products at bentonscountryhams2.com.) The dough, of course, ultimately makes the pizza, and this dough recipe will up your pizza game immediately.

BRUSSELS SPROUTS & BACON PIZZA

(MAKES 4 PERSONAL PIZZAS)

For the dough:

2½ teaspoons active dry yeast

1½ cups warm water

2 cups 00 flour or all-purpose flour

1 cup high-gluten flour or bread flour

2 teaspoons kosher salt

For the toppings:

1 pound bacon, sliced into 16 strips

1 pound Brussels sprouts

1 pound shredded provolone cheese

For the sauce:

3 tablespoons chopped garlic

⅛ teaspoon red pepper flakes

¼ cup bacon fat (or olive oil if preferred)

1 (35-ounce) can crushed tomatoes (San Marzano preferred)

1 teaspoon salt

⅓ cup chopped fresh parsley

2 tablespoons chopped fresh basil

To make the dough: Combine yeast and water in a bowl and stir to dissolve. Let sit 5–10 minutes, until yeast blooms and rises to the surface.

Add flours and salt. If using an electric mixer, use the dough hook attachment and mix on low for 4 minutes. Let dough rest 5 minutes, then mix on low for 4 more minutes.

If kneading by hand, lightly flour countertop and knead 200 strokes. Let dough rest 5 minutes, then knead 200 more strokes.

Let dough rise in a loosely covered container (cloth or foil) 1–3 hours, until tripled in size.

Divide into 4 equal portions and lightly flour. For each ball, fold the corners under, forming a smooth skin side on top. Keeping skin side up, continue folding under to create surface tension, until the dough becomes a smooth ball. Cover and let rest in refrigerator overnight.

To prepare the toppings: Cook bacon strips until they just begin to curl but are not yet browned. Chop in ¼-inch strips. Save bacon fat for sauce and Brussels sprouts.

Trim bottoms off Brussels sprouts and cut into quarters. Heat bacon fat on stove top, add sprouts, and cook on medium until soft and just starting to brown.

To make the sauce: Sauté garlic and pepper flakes in bacon fat until garlic is browned. Add tomatoes and salt. Gently simmer for 10 minutes.

Add herbs; gently simmer for 45 minutes more.

Refrigerate overnight or let cool before using.

To make the pizzas: Remove dough from refrigerator and let rest at room temperature 1 hour before using. Put a baking stone on top oven rack and turn on the broiler to heat for 1 hour before baking.

Stretch dough into 10-inch rounds.

Top with sauce first, then provolone, Brussels sprouts, and finally bacon.

Bake directly on stone under the broiler with oven door cracked open (to ensure broiler element stays on). When crust puffs up and back begins to brown, rotate pizza and continue cooking until crust is golden brown all around, 3–5 minutes.

THE NASHVILLE FARMER'S MARKET

If you expect our farmers' market to be just a place to buy produce, you're in for a surprise. The powerhouse Nashville Farmers' Market has grown to symbolize the best and most exciting food trends going on in the city. Oh yes, there are a crop of sellers who maintain regular stalls in the market daily, and a larger farm and artisan market, as well as a flea market, on weekends. But there's more to it than that.

Skirting Bicentennial Park in Germantown, just north of the state capitol grounds (and affording a wonderful view of the antebellum capitol building), the Nashville Farmers' Market also has a market house full of some of the most creative restaurants in Nashville, some of which are represented in this book: Bowl and Roil, Music City Crepes, B&C Market Barbecue, Bella Nashville, Chicago Gyro, El Burrito Mexicano, the incredibly popular Jamaicaway, The Original Nooley's Cajun cuisine, Swagruha, and many more grace the market house, where half the city comes for lunch.

There's an International Grocery, specializing in South Asian cooking supplies, and during the week a host of artisan bakers and other food purveyors sell their wares from tables in and out of the Market House. A bevy of plant sellers, many selling Tennessee-raised additions for gardens, thrive here, including the permanent Gardens of Babylon. The market has even added a micro-pub, The Picnic Tap, serving locally and regionally crafted beers and ciders.

The market is host to major events, from visits from popular cooking shows like *Top Chef* to chef-driven, hosted dinners featuring culinary experts from Nashville and beyond. Those events also have included the Southern Artisan Cheese Festival for several years and plenty of food charity–driven occasions.

Cities like New York, San Francisco, Portland, or Seattle may have had such options for a long time, but for us, the Nashville Farmers' Market is a major sign of the progress we've made, especially in the last decade, when it comes to our food community. The market is a bellwether for us, telling us where our food trends are going and reminding us that security in the food community is vital. Indeed, the Nashville Farmers' Market vendors serve some of the city's poorest, as well as its most affluent, every day. Many a restaurant meal begins at the market, and many a home-cooked one as well.

Visit nashvillefarmersmarket.org for more.

As it happens, in the years since this book first came out, farmers' markets have proliferated. I do most of my shopping at the Franklin Farmers' Market year-round, and love the newly local-to-me Murfreesboro Farmers' Market on the Square. I adore the delightful small market held at Murfreesboro's John Rice Agricultural Center early Tuesday and Friday mornings in the summer, full of local farmers, where I can zip in before work to grab the day's fresh tomatoes, strawberries and corn. New markets have appeared all over the area (Brentwood opened one in June 2018), and it makes it so much easier for all of us to shop seasonally and support our farmers. Visit picktnproducts.org for a complete list of area farmers' markets, to find one local to you. The state's Pick TN Products program does a wonderful job of promoting local growers and makers.

BISCUIT LOVE TRUCK

316 11th Avenue South, Nashville
(615) 490-9584
2001 Belcourt Avenue, Nashville
(615) 610-3336
132 3rd Avenue South, Franklin
biscuitlove.com
biscuitlovetruck.com

Since the last iteration of this book, Karl Worley's Biscuit Love has found brick and mortar premises down in the Gulch, and is easily one of the most popular destinations in town. And the food is still as wonderful and original as it was during his food truck start-up years. It's so good, he's opened Hillsboro Village and Franklin locations. I remember the very first time I tried the Princess Biscuit that Karl Worley of Biscuit Love has shared for this book. (The name pays homage to hot chicken icon Andre Prince of Prince's Hot Chicken.) I was at the Franklin Farmers' Market, out early, hadn't eaten breakfast, and was starving—and lo and behold, among the many excellent food vendors, I saw Biscuit Love (then using Jason McConnell's mobile food truck) and headed over. It only took the words "hot chicken" to sell me.

I sat at a picnic table, set my bag of produce next to me, and shot an image of my gorgeous biscuit, with its creamy, textured mustard and fresh pickles to upload to Facebook before I ate. The moment I bit into it, I knew I had something miraculous in my hands. Rich, homemade, grainy mustard and tart pickle hit my taste buds first, then the heat of the chicken, but not enough to make me call for water, like something from Prince's. It was just right, on every level. The use of the flavorful chicken thigh instead of breast meat made the tastes more complex.

Nashville has plenty of takes on our specialty hot chicken, but this is one of my very favorites.

Biscuit Love has plenty more to love, like the East Nasty, with buttermilk fried chicken, Kenny's farmhouse cheddar, and sausage gravy; and the Gertie, with homemade banana jam, peanut butter with pretzel crunch (they make it themselves), and Olive & Sinclair chocolate gravy. Oh, and grab a side of cheese grits while you're at it. Try it, feel the biscuit love.

THE PRINCESS BISCUIT

(SERVES 10)

For the chicken brine:

2 cups buttermilk

2 tablespoons kosher salt

2 tablespoons freshly ground black pepper

2 teaspoons granulated garlic

2 teaspoons granulated onion

2 tablespoons smoked paprika

10 boneless, skinless chicken thighs

For the biscuits:

1½ teaspoons rapid-rise dry yeast

¼ cup warm water (around 115°F)

4 teaspoons sugar, divided

2 cups soft winter wheat flour

2 teaspoons baking powder

½ teaspoon baking soda

1 teaspoon salt

⅓ cup butter plus ¼–⅓ cup butter, melted

1 cup full-fat buttermilk

For the fried chicken and dip:

Enough peanut oil for frying
  (1 cup reserved after frying for dip)

1 cup all-purpose flour

1 large egg

1 teaspoon baking powder

1 teaspoon smoked paprika

1 teaspoon salt

1 teaspoon pepper

1 teaspoon granulated garlic

1 teaspoon granulated onion

1½ cups water

10 tablespoons cayenne pepper

For assembly:

Honey

Creole mustard

Dill pickles slices

To brine the chicken: Mix all the ingredients except the chicken in a bowl. Add chicken and allow to brine overnight.

To make the biscuits: Mix yeast, water, and 2 teaspoons sugar in a large bowl and allow yeast to bloom for 30 minutes.

Whisk together flour, baking powder, baking soda, salt, and remaining 2 teaspoons of sugar. Add ⅓ cup butter, buttermilk, and yeast mixture to dry ingredients and stir with hands to just combine, being

careful not to overwork the dough. Cover dough and let rest in a warm area for 30 minutes to rise.

Place dough on a floured surface and roll it out to ¾ inch thick. Cut biscuits with biscuit cutter. Nestle together on a buttered sheet pan and brush tops with butter. Allow to rest and rise for 15 minutes. Meanwhile, preheat oven to 425°F.

Bake for 12 minutes, or until tops are golden brown. Remove from oven and brush immediately with remaining melted butter.

To prepare the fried chicken and dip: Add peanut oil to frying pan and place over heat. Using a deep-fry thermometer, heat the oil to 350°F.

Whisk all the ingredients except the cayenne pepper together.

Remove the chicken from the brine and dry with paper towels. Dip the chicken thighs into batter mixture and place chicken into hot oil, being careful not to overcrowd.

Fry for 7–8 minutes or until the internal temperature of the chicken reaches 165°F.

Remove 1 cup of oil from the oil used for frying the chicken, being careful not to spill, as it is very hot. Mix with cayenne pepper in a heatproof bowl. Dip chicken into mixture, and allow it to rest on a wire rack for 1 minute.

To assemble: Slice biscuits in half. Place chicken onto biscuit and top with honey, Creole mustard, and 3 dill pickle slices.

{brunch}
Easter Sunday 2013

Fontina Fondue 7
Garlic Potatoes, Herbs
Truffle Oil, Wine

BLVD NASHVILLE

2013 Belmont Boulevard, Belmont/Vanderbilt
(615) 385-2422
blvdnashville.com

Arnold Myint is the wunderkind of the Nashville food scene grown up. The Nashville native grew up dividing his time between here and South Asia, where his family originated. He made a first career as a competitive, then professional ice skater. Being from a family with a gift for food (his mother, Patti, owns and operates the wonderful International Market & Restaurant nearby), he's now parlayed his culinary talents not only into several of the city's best and most innovative eateries, but also into a place on *Top Chef* Season 7 and a host of other media appearances—with more coming.

In 2013 he closed his incredibly popular concept restaurant Cha-Cha and replaced it with BLVD, a bistro-style restaurant with a delightful menu of creative sandwiches, marvelous entrees (the Salmon 'n' Grits particularly), and an inventive chef's tasting menu. There's also a marvelous weekend brunch, featuring the likes of a Local Feta Omelet, Maple Waffle, Quinoa Cassoulet, and an excellent Croque Madame.

Myint's other locales, Suzy Wong's House of Yum downtown and PM, also in Belmont, are the kind of boutique gems you find yourself drawn to again and again, because Myint excels at that atmosphere.

I've long been a fan of Arnold's culinary skills, but you can't help appreciating his broad wit, his showmanship, and his dramatic talents as well. There's no one else quite like him in Nashville.

These Brussels sprouts are a perfect spicy side dish for a host of meals.

BRUSSELS SPROUTS

(YIELD DETERMINED BY COOK)

Chef Myint says, "This is a recipe that isn't standardized. I believe that the beauty of cooking is finding a balance based on your personal palate. Just remember, Thai chili peppers are spicy!"

Diced butter cubes

Roughly crushed Spanish Marcona almonds

Chopped Thai chili peppers

Thinly sliced red onion

White balsamic vinegar

Brussels sprout petals*

AM Smoked Salt (available at arnoldmyint.com/ shop)

Shaved Pecorino Romano

In a sauté pan, heat butter, almonds, Thai chili, and red onion. Allow butter to slightly brown and other components to sweat and slightly caramelize.

Deglaze the pan with vinegar and add the Brussels sprout petals. Toss the petals and sprinkle AM Smoked Salt as desired.

Remove from heat and finish with shaved Pecorino Romano.

*Note: In preparing your Brussels sprouts, pick the outer petals until you hit the center core. Sadly, in this process we do not use the center.

EDAMAME SALSA

(SERVES 4-6)

⅓ cup light soy sauce

⅓ cup rice vinegar

¼ cup olive oil

1 tablespoon sesame oil

1 cup granulated sugar

1 tablespoon Dijon mustard

2 cups shelled edamame (out of pods)

1 cup diced sweet white onion

1 cup diced tomato

½ cup sliced scallion

½ cup roughly chopped cilantro

2 tablespoons black and white sesame seeds

Whisk the soy sauce, vinegar, olive oil, sesame oil, sugar, and mustard together until sugar is dissolved.

Combine all the remaining ingredients in a mixing bowl. Add the dressing and store in the refrigerator until ready to serve.

BOB'S STEAK AND CHOP HOUSE

Omni Hotel, 250 Fifth Avenue South, Nashville
(615) 782-5300
omnihotels.com/hotels/nashville/dining/bobs-steak-and-chop-house

One of three exceptional locations for diners in the Omni, Bob's is a classic American steakhouse with a menu full of the kind of red meat and sides you imagine being the heart of country music cooking. If you're looking for a solid dose of high-quality Midwestern beef, this is an outstanding choice. With recognition by *Bon Appétit, Travel and Leisure, Nashville Lifestyles,* and a host of others, Bob's delivers a fine steakhouse experience. Travelers and locals alike make this place a dinner destination.

Look around and you'll see diners in suits and diners in jeans, all of whom are here to enjoy a calm ambiance and maybe a great cocktail. Bob's balances the bouncing energy of Barlines, and the traditional family energy of Kitchen Notes. If you want a private dining experience, book the Flag Room, which celebrates Americana in style.

Of course, beyond its land and sea proteins and delicious sides, Bob's also masters the whole lush dessert concept, as exemplified by this utterly marvelous piña colada cake.

PIÑA COLADA CHEESECAKE WITH COCONUT RUM CARAMEL
(SERVES 8-10)

Prep Time: 25 minutes

Necessary Tools:

10-inch springform pan

Medium-size stainless steel bowl

KitchenAid table-top mixer (or equivalent) with paddle attachment

High-temperature rubber spatula

Cooling rack

2-inch-deep baking dish

Large saucepan

For the crust:

2½ cups graham cracker crumbs

½ cup sugar

½ cup butter, melted

For the filling:

32 ounce cream cheese, softened

1¼ cup sugar

1 cup cream of coconut

½ cup dark rum

2½ teaspoons coconut extract

½ teaspoon salt

5 large eggs, lightly beaten

For the rum caramel:

1 cup sugar

¼ cup water

¼ teaspoon salt

¾ cup heavy cream

3½ tablespoons salted butter, cubed

¼ cup coconut rum

For the garnish:

Whipped cream

Toasted coconut flakes

Pineapple Jam (recipe follows)

Maraschino cherries

For the crust: Preheat the oven to 350°F. Lay two sheets of aluminum foil (approximately 20 x 20-inch) on top of each other. Place the spring form pan in the center of the foil and tightly wrap the outside of the pan with the foil up to the top of it.

In a medium-size stainless steel bowl, combine the graham cracker crumbs and the sugar and mix well. Stir in the melted butter and mix thoroughly. Once the crumb mixture is fully mixed, press it into the bottom of the pan and 1½ inches up the side of the pan. Make sure it is pressed smoothly.

Bake in the center of the oven for 10 minutes. Once done, pull out and cool on a wire rack, leaving the aluminum foil intact.

For the filling: Drop the oven temperature to 300°F. Using your table top mixing bowl, add in the softened cream cheese and sugar together. Turn the mixer on low and beat until smooth. Add in the cream of coconut and continue to mix. Add in the rum, coconut extract and the salt and mix.

Change the mixer speed to low, and slowly add in the eggs until just combined. Pour the finished mixture into the cooled crust.

Place the filled springform pan into the center of the baking dish and add in 1 inch of hot water.

Place into the 300°F oven and bake for 2 hours and 10 minutes or until the center is almost set.

Once the cake is cooked, pull the pan out of the water bath and cool for 30 minutes.

After 30 minutes, run a small sharp knife around the edges of the cheesecake to loosen it from the pan.

Continue to cool for at least 1 hour. Then refrigerate uncovered overnight.

For the caramel: Combine sugar, water and salt in a medium non-stick sauce pan and place on the stove on medium heat and bring to a boil. Allow to cook until it reaches an amber color.

Slowly add the cream to the sugar mixture because it will boil quickly. Keep on low heat and stir until smooth.

Remove from heat and add in the butter and the rum. Stir until fully incorporated.

Cool completely.

Store the caramel in the refrigerator until you need it. Serve at room temperature.

PINEAPPLE JAM

(SERVES 8–10)

1 pineapple

2 tablespoons lime juice

½ cup sugar

½ teaspoon salt

Peel and core pineapple, then dice it small.

Place all ingredients into a medium sauce pot and cook on low heat for about 30 minutes.

Cool completely.

BURGER UP

2901 12th Avenue South, 12South
(615) 279-3767
burger-up.com
401b Cool Springs Boulevard, Franklin
(615) 503-9892
burgerupcoolsprings.com

We got to know Miranda Whitcomb Pontes first with the coffee-centric restaurant Frothy Monkey in the 12South neighborhood before moving on to Burger Up, a burger concept restaurant that relies on sustainable, organic meats. When she created the concept, the movie *Food, Inc.* was freshly out and on everyone's minds, and she wanted an alternative to the factory farmed foods. The first thing on her agenda was to source the very best possible meats, and she did that via Williamson County's Triple L Ranch. She followed that up by sourcing other necessary products at a growing number of local farms in the Middle Tennessee area.

One of the fabulous things about Burger Up, of course, is the fact that not all the burgers are actually beef. They do a killer Citrus Salmon burger, for example, and a really great lamb burger. I must admit, I favor the old-school Woodstock, with Jack Daniel's maple ketchup.

But the pimento cheese–topped Ramsey Burger is a must-try. Pimento cheese is another long-time Southern favorite, and there's a wonderful story that makes it even better. Miranda first used the recipe for the "Mrs. Ida" on the menu at Frothy Monkey, then moved on to reimagine it as the Ramsey Burger at Burger Up.

"A dear friend's mother, Mrs. Ida Ramsey, from Viola, Tennessee, had a special pimento cheese recipe she kindly shared with me," says Miranda. "Mrs. Ida made all her recipes with love, wrote and published a number of cookbooks, and had a passion for feeding folks."

Pontes no longer owns the Franklin location, but they keep her style firmly embedded in their menu. She's added Josephine and Lulu, among other restaurant concepts, to the Nashville food scene, and continues to be a powerhouse in our food world.

THE RAMSEY BURGER

Assemble per person:

1 (5.5-ounce) burger patty, grilled medium
(Burger Up uses Triple L Ranch beef* 80/20.)

2 ounces Miss Ida's Pimento Cheese
(recipe follows)

Thinly sliced red onion

Bibb or butter lettuce

3–4 of your favorite pickle chips (the thicker
the better.)

Toasted bun

*Note: You may order Triple L Ranch beef at lllranch.com.

MISS IDA'S PIMENTO CHEESE

(YIELDS ENOUGH FOR AT LEAST 8 BURGERS)

1 pound grated (largest grate) yellow cheddar
    (Burger Up uses Sweetwater Valley.*)

⅔ cup mayonnaise (Duke's preferred)

2 tablespoons sour cream

3 tablespoons pickle juice (your favorite)

1 tablespoon hot sauce (your favorite)

¼ white onion, grated

Pinch of kosher salt

1 red bell pepper, grilled, peeled, and diced

Add all the ingredients to a bowl and mix with a wooden spoon or rubber spatula. Adjust seasoning (salt, pickle juice, or hot sauce) to your taste.

Note: Find Sweetwater Valley cheeses at sweetwatervalley.com.

Cabana Restaurant

1910 Belcourt Avenue, Hillsboro Village
(615) 577-2262
cabananashville.com

Cabana, one of the extraordinary restaurants under the auspices of Randy Rayburn, Craig Clift, and Brian Uhl, is a place you go for pure enjoyment. Set in Hillsboro Village within walking distance of Sunset Grill and plenty of other very good restaurants, Cabana ofers an awesome atmosphere and a marvelous menu, which is Southern comfort food made sleek and intriguing, given the creative talents of Uhl, whose expertise can't be understated.

The real fun is that much of the restaurant is divided into large, semiprivate booths, lushly cushioned and curtained, so that your party can enjoy a bit of private conversation and personal space. The concept works well, whether your goal is to have a business dinner or celebrate a little time with friends. You can bring a loaded iPod to dock or even watch the big game within your cabana while you sip on wine (it's an exceptional wine list, given the presence of Craig Clift).

Start out with the lump crab hush puppies or the coffee-and-cocoa-crusted venison carpaccio (always trust Uhl with game meats). When you get to dinner, the Tennessee rainbow trout or perhaps the peach barbecue pork shanks definitely appeal. Finish up with the daily cheesecake or cobbler selection.

Cabana thrives by being experiential—and you'll never regret a moment of it.

CRAB CAKES WITH ASIAN SLAW & MANGO CHILI SAUCE
(SERVES 4)

For the Asian slaw:

1 head Napa cabbage, sliced ½ inch thick

2 tablespoons sesame oil

1 cup sour cream

3 tablespoons sweet chili sauce

2 teaspoons rice wine vinegar

Salt and pepper to taste

For the crab cakes:

1 pound lump crab

1 red bell pepper, diced small

2 tablespoons sliced chives

1 lemon, juiced

1 teaspoon Dijon, or to taste

2–3 ounces mayonnaise

Salt and pepper to taste

3–4 tablespoons ground panko bread crumbs

1–2 tablespoons oil for frying

For the mango chili sauce:

1 cup mango puree

3 tablespoons sweet chili

1 teaspoon sambal chili or other hot chili sauce, to taste

To make the Asian slaw: Mix all the ingredients in a mixing bowl and refrigerate for at least an hour.

To make the crab cakes: Fold together all the ingredients for the crab cakes and form them into 3- to 4-ounce patties. Sauté in a nonstick pan with a little oil until golden brown on both sides.

To make the mango chili sauce: Mix all the ingredients together until well blended.

Plate crab cakes on the slaw, and drizzle with sauce before serving.

LOBSTER & BRIE "MAC AND CHEESE"
WITH BENTON'S SMOKY MOUNTAIN COUNTRY HAM CRISP
(SERVES 4)

While there are several traditional takes on the Southern standard macaroni and cheese in this book, this particular variation is quite unlike anything else—it makes use of rich, creamy brie, heavy cream, and Parmesan, paired with lobster meat for something deliciously decadent yet still in the realm of "comfort food." This is definitely the most grown-up method provided here for mac and cheese, and note they gave it to me with playful quotes around "mac and cheese"—this ain't your five-year-old's take on the dish, and that's as it should be. You can find Benton's Country Ham at bentonscountryhams2.com.

2 cups heavy cream

4 cups cooked ditalini pasta (or any small-cut macaroni)

Salt and black pepper to taste

5 ounces brie, cut into small cubes

1 ounce Parmesan cheese, freshly grated

8 ounces cooked lobster meat

8–10 slices Benton's Country Ham prosciutto (or your favorite prosciutto), sliced paper thin

1 teaspoon olive oil

2 tablespoons chopped chives, for garnish

In a large sauté pan, bring heavy cream to a boil. Add the cooked pasta and reduce cream by one-third. Season with salt and pepper. Stir in the cheeses and let it thicken, then add the lobster meat. Heat until the lobster is warmed through and the cheese is completely melted.

Brush the ham slices with olive oil and bake on a sheet pan for 6–8 minutes in a 350°F oven (or cook until the ham is crisp).

Spoon the "mac and cheese" onto a plate. Top with crispy country ham, sprinkle with chives, and garnish with a lobster claw.

caffé Nonna

4427 Murphy Road, Sylvan Park
(615) 463-0133
caffenonna.com

Caffé Nonna, a magical little neighborhood Italian restaurant located in Sylvan Park, offers delicious comfort food. A little off busier West End, the area boasts wonderful vintage homes and cottages appealing to young families. Within the walls of Caffé Nonna, locals and nonlocals alike converge to consume incredible pasta dishes and wood-fired pizzas.

Start out your order with the Tuscan Bruschetta or Mussels Apulia, then move on perhaps to a Nonna Salad with fried calamari added or a larger meal—the Seafood Angelini is popular, and so is the Lasagna Nonna. Or you can go for a pizza, from a basic Margherita to the limits of your imagination with a plethora of delicious add-ons. There's quite a respectable wine list, too.

When ordering pasta, you can choose your pasta type, sauce, and additions as well. Better yet, take a jar of the marvelously spicy arrabiata (I always order this one) or regular marinara home with you. In doing so, you support the Zoe Marie Foundation, a Partner in Hope with St. Jude's Children's Hospital. Named for Chef Dan's lovely daughter in memory of her tragic struggle with brain cancer, the Zoe Marie Foundation marries fantastic foods with the best of causes. (You can order these sauces and other products from Chef Dan and Caffe Nonna wherever you are, via nonnasgourmetfoods.com.)

SMOKED SALMON WITH ORECCHIETTE PASTA

(SERVES 4-6)

1 pound orecchiette pasta

¼ small red onion, sliced thin

3 plum tomatoes, seeded and diced

2 tablespoons chopped garlic

½ cup capers

Olive oil for sautéing

8 ounces smoked salmon, rolled and
   sliced into strips

¼ cup grainy mustard

1 cup white wine

¾ cup mascarpone

¼ cup chopped dill

4 cups baby arugula

Kosher salt, to taste

Cracked black pepper, to taste

¼ cup basil, cut into thin strips,
   for garnish

Fill up a pot with enough cold water to cook the pasta. Add some salt to it and let it come to a boil. Cook pasta per package instructions once you get the sauce going. Then strain and toss in a little bit of olive oil so it doesn't stick.

In a large sauté pan on medium-high heat, add the onion, tomato, garlic, capers, and olive oil. Sauté for 3-4 minutes, stirring to blend. Scrape the bottom to release the bits of flavor to create the foundation of the sauce.

Add the smoked salmon and grainy mustard. Sauté another 1-2 minutes. Pour in the white wine and reduce by one-fourth. Add the mascarpone and stir to combine. Reduce for 2–3 minutes, longer if needed, to slightly thicken.

Add the pasta, dill, and arugula. Heat through and toss to combine. Taste and season with salt and pepper. You can add a bit more wine to thin out and stretch the sauce if necessary. The sauce should cling to the pasta.

Portion the pasta onto plates and garnish with the basil, and cheese if you like.

THE BLOOMY RIND

One sign of growth in the local food community is indubitably the proliferation of artisan foods in Middle Tennessee. Kathleen Cotter started her Bloomy Rind artisan cheese shop inside local organic Porter Road Butcher, in East Nashville. Since the first edition of this book, Cotter has turned the retail portion of Bloomy Rind over to Porter Road, where it remains a remarkable cheese counter, and expanded her wholesale work to encompass the area's rising demand for extraordinarily special cheeses. Her efforts ensure the cheese plates of many local restaurants remain something special when they leave the kitchen.

Cotter started out in human resources, but a few years ago decided she was ready to shift gears and contemplated where her passions lay. "It came down to cheese and chocolate," she says. At

that time, Scott Witherow of Olive & Sinclair was making waves in the chocolate world, so Cotter went for cheese. After a sabbatical spent learning about the American artisan cheese movement, including cheese boot camp at Murray's in New York City, she set herself up as a cheesemonger. She hawked fine cheeses privately, including fine representations of Southern cheesemaking, at the Nashville Farmers' Market.

Cotter focused on representative Southern products like Green Hill from Georgia's Sweet Grass Dairy and a few others that really struck her, some outside our region (the South traditionally hasn't had an artisan cheese culture). "Ascutney Mountain [Cobb Hill Cheese, Vermont], a magical alpine-style cheese, was an early favorite of mine," she says. "And Barely Buzzed [Beehive Cheese Co., Utah] is such a strange, delicious concept with a coffee and lavender rub on the rind. Then came Wisconsin's Dunbarton Blue (Roelli Cheese), a natural rind cheddar with bits of blue in it, which led to more, and more." As her interest grew, business thrived.

Also known for creating the successful annual Southern Artisan Cheese Festival, which had huge impact on our local cheese perspective for several years, Kathleen Cotter continues to show local residents and restaurants how to do cheese just right.

The Bloomy Rind Cheese Counter (retail), 501 Gallatin Avenue; (615) 429-9648

The Bloomy Rind (wholesale), (781) 740-1001; bloomyrind.com

CAPITOL GRILLE

231 6th Avenue North (Hermitage Hotel), Downtown
(615) 345-7116
capitolgrillenashville.com

A lot of the credit for changing the farm-to-fork ethos in Nashville goes to the chefs and business decisions made by the Capitol Grill over the past few years, starting with Chef Tyler Brown and continuing through to today's staff. The folks at Capitol Grille and the Hermitage Hotel have brought about a paradigm shift in terms of showing the public what sustainability and land preservation are all about. They have spent the past several years developing a vast garden at the Land Trust for Tennessee's farm at Glen Leven. Here, they've worked tirelessly to raise a huge percentage of the produce used at the Capitol Grille, inspiring others to follow suit as they go.

Recently the hotel invested in a 245-acre property, Double H Farms, to build on their sustainability commitment. Here they'll continue to raise cattle, honey, and a variety of crops destined for a place at your table at the Capitol Grille.

The ongoing awareness of the food as part of the land translates, into an understanding of cookery that means every meal at the Capitol Grille is something special.

My husband and I have enjoyed many a dinner at the Capitol Grille—it's the kind of place where you can look around and see celebrities, tourists, politicians, and mostly regular people, all of whom are there to appreciate the fine food. The bar is set high on everything, and whether you just want old-fashioned fried chicken or something more elaborate, you'll be pleased with the result.

HANGER STEAK WITH VEGETABLE FRITES & DOUBLE-FRIED FRENCH FRIES

(SERVES 8)

Chimichurri

⅓ cup extra-virgin olive oil

1 clove garlic, peeled and finely chopped or pressed

1 cup parsley leaves, well-rinsed, lightly packed

1 cup cilantro leaves, well-rinsed, lightly packed

1 teaspoon salt

¼ teaspoon freshly ground black pepper

1 tablespoon sherry vinegar

¼ cup minced red onion (or add chunks to food processor before herbs)

1 tablespoon capers, rinsed

In a small food processor, combine the olive oil and garlic and run until the garlic is well distributed. (If you don't feel like mincing the onion by hand, you can add it in chunks now, but it won't look as nice.) If you don't have a small food processor, you might need to make a double batch, as a full-size machine probably won't work well on this small quantity.

Add the parsley, cilantro, salt, pepper, and vinegar and process until minced but with still a bit of texture left in the leaves.

Remove from the food processor and mix in the onions and capers.

Let rest at least 30 minutes, then taste and adjust salt, pepper, and vinegar as needed.

Hanger Steak

4 pounds trimmed hanger steak

⅓ cup chimichurri (recipe provided)

Marinate the hanger steak overnight with chimichurri (reserve remainder for later use).

Vegetable Frites

1 fennel bulb, cut into 8 wedges

16 baby carrots, peeled or cleaned with a wet towel

16 pearl onions

1 large celery root, peeled and cut into batonettes

1 cup water

1 cup rice wine vinegar

1 cup sugar

2 bay leaves

3 sprigs thyme

½ teaspoon salt

Olive oil for drizzling

Preheat oven to 350°F.

Combine all the ingredients in a Dutch oven with the lid, bring to a boil on stovetop, then braise in the oven for 1 hour.

Remove from oven and allow vegetables to cool in the liquid.

Remove the vegetables from the liquid and reserve liquid for another use. Pat the veggies dry, then lay them on a baking sheet that has been drizzled with olive oil.

Bake at 350°F, until crispy. Reseason with salt, pepper, and herbs if you like.

Double-Fried French Fries

1 pound Kennebec potatoes

1 pound sweet potatoes

2 quarts canola oil

1 tablespoon fine-grain sea salt

1 teaspoon freshly ground black pepper

Peel potatoes on the sides, leaving the ends with the skin on. Cut the potatoes into ⅓-inch slices and then slice into ⅓-inch sticks.

Fill a large bowl with water and soak potatoes, submerged, for at least 30 minutes and up to 24 hours. This will help remove the excess starch from the potatoes and keep them from oxidizing.

Heat oil in a heavy stockpot fitted with a deep-fry thermometer to 325°F.

Remove potatoes from the water, and pat dry to remove excess water. Add 2 handfuls of potatoes to hot oil. There should be at least 1 inch of oil above the potatoes. Par-cook until potatoes are light brown, 5–7 minutes. Remove potatoes, gently shaking off excess oil, and let drain on rack. Repeat until all of the potatoes are par-cooked.

Raise heat of oil to 350°F.

Cook potatoes again, 2 handfuls at a time, until golden brown, about 2 minutes. Remove from oil, shake off excess oil, and season lightly in a bowl with salt and pepper. Repeat until all potatoes are cooked.

Plating the dish: Grill the hanger steak to preferred doneness. Crisp up the Vegetables Frites by sautéing lightly in olive oil. French fries should ideally be made right before serving. Arrange on the plate and garnish the steak with the remaining chimichurri.

SALAD WITH GREEN GODDESS DRESSING

(MAKES ABOUT 2 PINTS DRESSING)

A flavorful side dish with any meal, especially beef or fish.

5 cloves garlic

1 shallot

1 tablespoon goat cheese

3 tablespoons Dijon mustard

2 ounces white wine vinegar

Juice of 1 lemon

5 egg yolks

4 anchovies

2 tablespoons chopped fresh parsley

1 tablespoon rough-chopped fresh tarragon

1 cup blended oil

Salad greens

Combine garlic, shallot, goat cheese, Dijon, white wine vinegar, lemon juice, anchovies, and yolks in a blender. Once smooth, add the herbs and emulsify the oil into it.

Drizzle dressing directly on salad greens.

SAUTÉED SWISS CHARD

(SERVES 8)

Greens tend to be available for a large portion of the year in Tennessee, and often we're at a loss for how to serve them creatively. This method for Swiss chard really emphasizes the full flavor of both leaves and stems and will have you wanting seconds of your vegetables.

2 pounds Swiss chard

4 teaspoons butter, divided

⅛ teaspoon pepper

½ teaspoon salt

1 tablespoon vinegar or lemon juice

Rinse chard and separate the stems from leaves. Cut stems into 2-inch pieces; cut leaves crosswise into 1-inch strips.

In a saucepan, add 2 teaspoons butter. Add chard stems to pan and sauté about 5 minutes. Add leaves and cook another 5 minutes. Add remaining 2 teaspoons butter and pepper.

Mound the chard in the center of a serving plate and drizzle with vinegar or lemon juice.

SPRING TROUT

(SERVES 8-10)

Tennessee is landlocked, and much ado is made about getting fresh fish in Nashville. These days it's reasonable to expect that our fine-dining establishments have had their seafood flown in directly from the coasts, and that it will be fresh. However, we also have the advantage of plenty of lakes and rivers; because of that, freshwater fish abound, and the possibilities for cooking them are

endless. This particular trout recipe will be appreciatively received by anyone who's a trout fan. If you wish to use the Capitol Grille trout source, you can order from Sunburst Trout Farms in North Carolina via sunbursttrout.com/products.

2 cups hominy

1 tablespoon salt

1 teaspoon black pepper

½ cup dry-roasted peanuts

8–10 trout fillets (Capitol Grille uses Sunburst Trout Farms trout.)

4 ounces peanut oil

Lightly roast the hominy on a cookie sheet in a 400°F oven for about 30 minutes, stirring twice. Place the roasted hominy, salt, pepper, and peanuts in a food mill (KitchenAid preferred) and dial the setting to coarse grind. Dredge the trout in the seasoned hominy mixture, then shallow-fry the fish to golden brown in peanut oil.

BLUEBERRY COBBLER COCKTAIL

The Oak Bar at the Hermitage Hotel is known for its astonishingly wonderful cocktails. A couple years ago, Tyler Brown set a precedent by arranging for single-barrel whiskey direct from the Jack Daniel's distillery in Lynchburg, Tennessee, and the resultant cocktails were amazing. There's nothing that comes out of the Oak Bar that doesn't dazzle. In this case, they've sent over a cocktail recipe that will appeal not only in spring, but in all seasons, in spite of its spring-like name. Of course, fresh local blueberries will always make this the best possible beverage, and when I told them I wanted a locally based cocktail, they went straight to the berries.

2 ounces Hangar One Straight Vodka

1 tablespoon opal basil leaves

½ ounce simple syrup

¾ ounce St. Germain elderflower liqueur

Juice of 1 lemon wedge

2–3 ice cubes

1 tablespoon blueberries

½–1 ounce soda

Shake together all ingredients except blueberries and soda with ice cubes to chill.

Pour soda and place blueberries in a martini or rocks glass. Strain cocktail ingredients into the glass over berries and serve.

carter's

Union Station Hotel, 1001 Broadway, Nashville
(615) 726-1001
unionstationhotelnashville.com/eat-drink

Carter's is the newest addition to Union Station, and whether you're local or a tourist it's a welcome respite from the bustle of downtown. Located close by the Frist Center and other popular attractions, it makes a wonderful stop for breakfast, lunch, or dinner. If you happen to be staying in the hotel, it provides a good argument not to leave at all when it comes to searching for a meal. The signature cocktails mean happy hour is a definite option as well.

The view and the ambiance at Union Station are truly magnificent. Having worked across the street at Gannett for years not long ago, I can attest to it being one of the most ideally placed locations in the city. More than once our staff made a cheerful pilgrimage across the street, or met up after an opening at the Frist Center.

Carter's replaces Prime 108, which was the pride of Union Station during the first edition of this book. While I'll miss Prime, this is a great factor in the renovation and refurbishment of the hotel, and I suspect diners will agree wholeheartedly. The atmosphere is more contemporary, the vibe both all-American and Southern. Union Station was converted from the city's old train station back in the '80s, and it still has the vibe of an elegant escape from the hustle of the day—and rail travel. The combination of old and new works visually and aesthetically throughout the hotel, and indeed, the restaurant.

The menu features small plates as well as larger entrées, and the popcorn treat that follows here pairs gloriously with beer or cocktails—or a glass of prosecco.

BACON BOURBON SALTED CARAMEL POPCORN
(SERVES 4-6)

4 ounces bacon

⅓ cup unpopped popcorn kernels

4 ounces unsalted butter, at room temperature, cut into pieces

¾ cup firmly packed light brown sugar

¼ cup light corn syrup

¼ cup bourbon plus 1 tablespoon

1 teaspoons kosher salt, plus extra as needed

½ teaspoon vanilla

½ teaspoon baking soda

½ cup blanched peanuts, lightly toasted

Cayenne, to taste (optional)

Position oven racks in upper and lower third of oven. Preheat oven to 250°F. Line two rimmed baking sheets with aluminum foil or parchment paper; set aside.

Lightly coat a very large bowl with nonstick spray. Lightly coat a large spoon or rubber spatula with nonstick spray; set aside.

Cook the bacon until crisp, in batches as needed, reserving fat. Drain bacon on paper towels and cool, then chop into tiny pieces; set aside. Strain fat, leaving any solids behind to discard.

Place bacon fat in a large, deep stockpot (at least a

Carter's **47**

6-quart pot) and place over low heat. Add a couple of corn kernels, cover and wait for them to pop. Add remaining popcorn and continue cooking over low heat until all the kernels are popped, shaking the pan a few times and lifting the lid once or twice to allow steam to escape. Pour popcorn into prepared bowl.

Place the butter, brown sugar, corn syrup, ¼ cup bourbon and salt in a heavy-bottomed, medium-size saucepan and stir to combine. Cook over medium-high heat until it boils, then boil for about 4 minutes without stirring. If you have a candy thermometer, you want the mixture to come to 275°F; the color should be a rich golden brown. Remove from the heat, add remaining 1 tablespoon bourbon, vanilla, and baking soda and swirl the pot to incorporate.

Immediately and slowly pour the caramel over the popcorn, stirring and tossing it constantly with the prepared spoon/spatula. You want to coat the popcorn as evenly as possible with the caramel. Toss in the bacon pieces as you go followed by the peanuts. Taste the popcorn at this stage. If you want more salt, or want to add cayenne to taste, sprinkle over the popcorn as you toss it.

Spread the mixture onto the baking sheets and cook in the oven; make sure you grease your pans. Cook the mixture for 30 minutes and stir well every 10 minutes to mix in caramel and to keep it coated. Cool the finished product and enjoy.

Union Station Hotel

CHAUHAN ALE & MASALA HOUSE

123 12th Avenue North, Nashville
(615) 242-8426
chauhannashville.com

How much raving do I get to do about Chef Maneet Chauhan and the changes she's wrought in the Nashville food community along with her husband Vivek Deora and her business associates? If I can pick any point at which more ethnic dining became a thing in Nashville, it was with her arrival and her evident reminders that the food of the South can be effortlessly blended with world flavors to create something wholly new and yet familiar. The city's food tastes shifted seismically—suddenly, even those with the most ordinary of tastes want to give all things Asian a go. Now, every suburb and bedroom community in the area is more excited than ever about all our Indian restaurants—and other non-US style dining.

Additionally, she partnered with Kayleigh and Derrick Morse to open Mantra Artisan Ales in Franklin, in Turtle Anarchy's old location. You can find the details of Mantra elsewhere in this book, but suffice to say, Nashville's beer culture has positively changed too. As a partner with Deora and others in Morph Hospitality, she's also supported other chefs, the result being the likes of Tànsuǒ, also found in this book.

This recipe underlines the Nashville-Asian fusion going on at Maneet Chauhan's hands—it's one of my favorites when they serve it at Chauhan, and I'm looking forward to trying this take on hot chicken myself at home.

HOT CHICKEN PAKORAS

(SERVES 6-8)

For the marinade:

2 pounds boneless, skinless chicken breasts (cut into 2 x 2-inch pieces)

1 quart buttermilk

2 tablespoons garlic ginger paste

2 teaspoons salt

1 teaspoon hing (also called asafoetida)

1 teaspoon cayenne

1 teaspoon freshly ground black pepper

1 teaspoon chili powder

½ teaspoon paprika

For the spice salt:

1 part chat masala

1 part jalapeño salt

½ part cayenne

½ part chipotle powder

1 part dried mint

For the hot sauce:

2500 grams habaneros

1000 grams yellow peppers

100 grams salt

75 grams orange peel

2 quarts champagne vinegar

1 cup honey

5 grams guar

Salt (optional)

For the pakora batter

1 cup chickpea flour

1 cup all-purpose flour

200 grams red chili powder

1 teaspoon hing/asafoetida

1 tablespoon salt

Soda water or club soda

1 tablespoon garlic ginger paste

To prepare the marinade: Mix all the marinade ingredients. Marinate the chicken for at least 2-3 hours in the marinade (preferably overnight).

To prepare the spice salt: Mix all ingredients and pass through a kitchen strainer or tammy. You will use about 1 teaspoon (and save the rest for another time).

To prepare the hot sauce: Blend habaneros, peppers, salt, and orange peel together. Ferment for 24 hours at room temperature. Pass the mash through a strainer to get maximum extraction. Blend in honey and vinegar. In small batches blend in guar to thicken. Season with salt if needed.

To prepare the pakora batter: Combine all dry ingredients in a medium-size mixing bowl. Whisk in the soda water until mixture reaches a smooth milkshake consistency. Finish by whisking in the garlic ginger paste.

For pick up: Dust the marinated chicken in flour. Shake off the excess flour and dip the chicken in the batter. Deep fry in a fryer at 350°F for 5 minutes or until chicken is cooked. Combine ingredients to your liking and enjoy!

Chef's Market Café & Takeaway

900 Conference Drive, Goodlettsville
(615) 851-2433
chefsmarket.com

Chef's Market has a stellar reputation as a caterer in the area, but they also have a restaurant worth visiting. The business started with the restaurant, and owners Jim and Cheryl Hagy almost immediately found themselves in demand as caterers—and a dual business began. Having been to events they catered and eaten in at the premises, I can say both stand out for simple, cleanly imagined, thoughtful dishes. The Nashville Scene has named them best caterer at least five times in recent memory—and *Scene* readers are demanding of their restaurants. Located on the north side of town in Goodlettsville, this is not just a restaurant to visit, but the place to call when you're in town for something like a bridal shower and need to call a caterer for your AirBnB crowd.

This salad speaks to exactly the type of dish you'll find at Chef's Market—fresh ingredients combined in a way that makes the flavor of each stand out and blend at the same time. The vinaigrette is incredibly easy to make in your home, and this is a winner whether you're serving two or having ten guests in for dinner.

ALPINE AVOCADO SALAD

(SERVES 6)

**For the avocado vinaigrette
(makes 10 ounces)**

1 avocado, peeled, seed removed

½ cup olive oil

⅔ cup water

2 tablespoon rice vinegar

1 bunch of green onion, no whites

½ teaspoon fresh garlic

¼ teaspoon sea salt

Place all ingredients in a blender, blend until smooth.

For the salad:

6 cups baby greens

2 avocadoes, diced

3 oranges (blood oranges if in season), peeled and segmented, white pith removed

2 ounces roasted pistachios

4 ounces goat cheese crumbles

Place greens in large bowl. Toss with half of dressing. Divide greens among six plates. Add ⅔ of the orange segments to bowl; toss with remaining dressing. Garnish with remaining orange segments and pistachios.

Chef's Market Café & Takeaway   **55**

CITY HOUSE

1222 4th Avenue North, Germantown
(615) 736-5838
cityhousenashville.com

City House is one of my favorite places in town, and I simply don't get there often enough since it's in Germantown, well north of my Franklin home. That's a pity, because Tandy Wilson serves up some of the best, most innovative food in Nashville. He tends to eschew personal publicity, but that hasn't kept him and City House from national note, everywhere from fashion and culture magazines to nominations for James Beard Awards, simply because of his talent and his creativity in the kitchen.

I first met Tandy at a party in Patrick Martin's home kitchen, as he strode through with a plate full of strips of meat, fresh from the grill, proffering it to fellow guests. I tried it, so did my husband—it was delicious. "What is it?" I asked.

"Pig's heart," replied Tandy, without a trace of a smile. From that moment he joined the small list of people (Tyler Brown, Jason McConnell, and himself) that have taught me to eat what they give me without even asking what it is on the plate.

At City House you'll find everything on the menu from oxtail stew to octopus pasta to more simple dishes such as the pork meatballs, and I recommend all of it. They also easily have one of the best bars in Nashville, the kind of bar where you don't mind going in alone, sitting on a stool, and ordering wine, cocktails, and dinner alone—someone you know will show up eventually, and if they don't, you won't care.

Every cocktail at City House is extraordinary as well (the wine list is also very good), and among them this offering stands out. Made with Corsair gin, which is a true juniper and citrus lover's gin, with a hint of grapefruit note, it's guaranteed to make you happy on a warm summer night.

PORCH POUNDER

1½ ounces Corsair Artisan Gin*

1½ ounces Martini and Rossi Roscato Vermouth

1 ounce lemon juice

¼ ounce Lazzaroni Amaretto

2 dashes Fee Bros. Rhubarb Bitters**

Splash of soda

Lemon slices for garnish

Build this drink in a pint jar, top it with soda, gently rotate the glass in your hand to lightly mix together the components, and serve with a lemon wheel to garnish.

*Note: You can find Corsair gin and products from the Corsair Artisan microdistillery in most major cities; find out more at corsairartisan.com.

**Note: Do not substitute! Omit if you don't have Fee Bros. Rhubarb Bitters. They can be found at many online gourmet sources and Amazon.com.

CITY WINERY

609 Lafayette Street, Nashville
(615) 324-1010
citywinery.com

City Winery is a local A-list entertainment venue, although part of a larger concept, that offers terrific meals and house-aged wines for a distinctive experience in each of its locales. Nashville's incarnation is very much unique to Music City and has established itself in less than five years as part of our culture—both in music and food. I tend to go when my burlesque performer friends, including Freya West and Shan de Leers of Delinquent Debutants are onstage, but there's almost always a stellar concert going on or an event worth attending, from holiday specials to charity-driven happenings.

The menu showcases the rustic side of the Mediterranean, with Italian, French, Spanish, and Middle-Eastern cultures—the idea being they all combined exquisite food culture with wine for centuries—make that millennia. The concept promotes meals that are wine inspired and regionally influenced with a dose of local sourcing, and some original takes on the larger vision of intertwining of food with wine.

They've opted to start us out with a classic grappa cocktail, and move on to a burrata with a touch of Southern US flair.

SOUR GRAPES GRAPPA COCKTAIL

2 ounces Rhinehall Grappa

1 ounce fresh squeezed lemon juice

1 ounce simple syrup

Egg white

Lemon slice for garnish

Mix all ingredients except lemon thoroughly, serve in a rocks glass. Garnish with a lemon

SOUTHERN BURRATA

So, you want the most glorious cheese ball you have ever eaten? Prepare to make one for yourself! Burrata isn't typically filled with pimento cheese, but it works brilliantly and makes it *soooo* very Nashville. Serve it with fresh local tomatoes for an amazing take on a caprese salad.

For the pimento cheese

2 cups shredded extra-sharp cheddar cheese

8 ounces cream cheese, softened

½ cup mayonnaise

¼ teaspoon garlic powder

¼ teaspoon ground cayenne pepper

¼ teaspoon onion powder

1 jalapeño pepper, seeded and minced

1 tablespoon Gochujang paste

1 (4-ounce) jar diced pimento, drained

Salt and black pepper to taste

For the homemade mozzarella:

⅓ cup non-fat dry milk powder for 7 pints of milk (read the label on the powdered milk because this can vary)

1 pint heavy cream

1½ teaspoons citric acid

¼ rennet tablet or ¼ teaspoons single strength liquid rennet

1 teaspoon salt

Making mozzarella curd: To make the milk, mix cream with dry milk powder for one gallon of milk. In a separate bowl, add rennet tablet or measure liquid rennet into ¼ cup of cool water and set aside. Allow rennet to dissolve in water.

Pour citric acid into a 1-cup measure of cool water.

Make sure this is stirred until it all dissolves.

Pour the citric acid solution into the cold pot and then quickly pour the milk on top of this. It is very important to stir well to prevent any localized coagulation, which will appear as curds float to the surface. There should be little to no curds forming at this stage.

Heat the milk slowly at medium heat to 90–92°F. Stir well enough to keep the milk from sticking or scorching.

At 90–92°F add the dissolved rennet water and stir for 20–30 seconds. Allow the milk to rest at this temperature totally still for coagulation. Initial firming of the milk will take place at about 2–2½ minutes, but allow the milk to firm a full 7–10 minutes before cutting.

Once the curds form, cut them into a checkerboard pattern of 1-inch square (larger for moister mozzarella). Wait 1–2 minutes, then very gently (curd is very soft at this point) cut horizontal layers with ladle or spoon. Result should be as equal in size as you can manage.

Once the curd forms well and seems to be releasing whey, it is time to separate the curds from whey. Allowing the curds to settle and consolidate for a minute or 2 will initially separate the whey.

The excess whey that rises can be poured off while holding the curds back with your hand. The curds should now be carefully transferred to a bowl with a spoon or perforated ladle (best). Pulling the curd back to the center of the bowl can now do further whey separation. You will see more whey running off at this point and this should be removed. Once the curd begins to consolidate well it is time to heat the curds to develop the stretching character of mozzarella.

Stretching the curd: Simmer some water to about 175°F, then pour water into a separate bowl.

Cut or break the curd into 1- to 2-inch pieces and begin placing them into the hot water.

As the curd begins to meld together, pull it from the hot water and begin to stretch it. If the curd does not stretch check and adjust your water temperature and reimmerse the curd.

Stretch it out several times and fold it back on itself and repeat. If it begins to cool too much (you will notice it begin to tear), place it back in the hot water to reheat.

To prepare the pimento cheese: Place the cheddar cheese, cream cheese, mayonnaise, garlic powder, cayenne pepper, onion powder, minced jalapeño, Gochujang, and pimento into the large bowl of a mixer. Beat at medium speed, with paddle if possible, until thoroughly combined. Season to taste with salt and black pepper.

To make the burrata: Repeat the stretching method with the mozzarella curd until you have formed a large ball. Cut off a Ping-Pong-ball-size piece with the scissors, stretch into a 6-inch round (like a pizza) and place inside the small soup bowl. We used a mold, but a bowl will work fine.

With string close by, place 3 ounces of pimento cheese mix in the middle of the mozzarella and gather sides up on the top.

Gently tie the top with the string like a small purse and place in ice bath. (this will help retain the shape). Repeat with the second ball and remainder of the curd/mixture.

BUTCHERY

NASHVILLE BUTCHER SCENE

Local butchers have become *de rigeur* in Nashville, whether you want charcuterie or a good steak from a local farm. Here are three you want to keep in mind when you're sourcing meats for your kitchen.

Porter Road Butcher

501 Gallatin Avenue, Nashville, TN 37206; (855) 877-8202

Porter Road Butcher was our first real artisan butcher shop, and they're still going strong. The brainchild of James Peisker and Chris Carter, a couple of guys looking for better ways to source local meats for area kitchens—restaurant and home. The storefront has grown to a significant online business as well for locally produced beef, poultry, and pork, processed in Porter Road's own Kentucky facility. The space also includees the cheese counter formally known as the Bloomy Rind, and still containing Kathleen Cotter's excellent and sought-after wares. Visit them at porterroad.com.

Carnivore

230 Franklin Road #12F, Franklin, TN 37064; (615) 614-3134

My husband and his work friends discovered Carnivore in the Factory at Franklin one afternoon after their mid-day workout. Seth came home with steaks and streaky bacon, and life has never been the same (at least for our grill). Carnivore specializes in charcuterie and hand-made sausages, but they also have a plentiful supply of carefully selected fresh beef, pork, and poultry—grass-fed, grain-fed, and antibiotic- and hormone-free. The treat of the moment to try is South African—style beef biltong (the owner grew up in South Africa). Visit online at carnivoremeatco.com.

Bare Bones Butcher

906 51st Avenue North, Nashville, TN 37209; (615) 730-9808

The new kid on the (butcher's) block, Bare Bones set up shop in The Nations, a growing Nashville neighborhood. They specialize in whole animal, local butchery, incluing beef, pork, poultry, and other options. Bare Bones also does more than just meat—they provide a splendid market for locally produced foodstuffs, including Bells Bend Farm, Charpier's Bakery, Giving Thanks Farm, Hatcher Dairy, Matchless Coffee, Sounding Stone Farms, Sugar Camp Farms, TruBee Honey, and Village Provisions Bakery. They do small market very well.

THE COCOA TREE

thecocoatree.com

I first met Bethany Torino when she had a lovely, tiny shop in Franklin where she was redefining what artisan chocolate was for the residents of Williamson County who were used to the stuff they bought at chain markets. I used to stop by regularly for chocolate espresso beans and a chance to check out whatever she was doing new. These days, she works primarily as a caterer and freelance professional, but the Cocoa Tree name follows her. Luckily for us, her products can be found at Fresh Market locations and other local retailers.

Bethany has received plenty of media attention for her exquisite handmade truffles, including those inspired by music artists who work in Nashville. She's worked with CMT Television, creating signature truffles paying tribute to the honorees for CMT Artist of the Year Awards. She created sweet treats using the inspiration of everyone from Carrie Underwood to the Zac Brown Band. Each one possesses elements that reflect the personality and work of the artist.

When asked to participate in this project, Bethany thoughtfully provided recipes for truffles inspired by two of the city's favorites, Oprah Winfrey and Amy Grant.

AMY'S BALSAMIC RASPBERRY TRUFFLES

Inspired by Amy Grant
"The one who knows the bitter and the sweet."
(MAKES 28 17-GRAM TRUFFLES)

8 ounces dark chocolate (72% cocoa content)

½ cup heavy cream

2 tablespoons raspberry puree

2 tablespoons balsamic vinegar

1 pound dark chocolate (for dipping)

¼ cup dried raspberries (for topping)

See "To Make the Truffles" on the next page.

SOFIA'S SWEET POTATO TRUFFLES

Inspired by Oprah Winfrey
"The one who's good for the soul."
(MAKES 34 17-GRAM TRUFFLES)

8 ounces milk chocolate (41% cocoa content)

¼ cup heavy cream

¼ cup sweet potato puree (recipe follows)

1 pound milk chocolate (for dipping)

1 ounce dried sweet potato curls (for topping)

For the sweet potato puree:

¼ cup heavy cream

½ cup baked sweet potato

¼ teaspoon nutmeg

¼ teaspoon cinnamon

To make the sweet potato puree: In a saucepan, bring cream just to a boil. Spoon baked sweet potato into a blender. Add cream, nutmeg, and cinnamon and blend until smooth.

To make the ganache: Bring 2 cups of water just to a boil in a 2½-quart saucepan. Place chocolate inside a glass or stainless bowl that fits just inside the saucepan. Melt the chocolate over the steam until it reaches 100°F. Remove the bowl from the steam.

Bring the heavy cream just to a boil and pour it immediately into the melted chocolate, stirring vigorously until the mixture is silky smooth.

At this time add your other ingredients to create exciting flavors. Amy uses purees, spices, liqueurs, and so on to bring her truffles to life: balsamic vinegar and raspberries or sweet potato puree in the case of these two truffles.

Refrigerate the ganache until it has the consistency of pudding. This should take at least 20 minutes. Then beat the ganache with a hand mixer for 15 seconds. Let the ganache rest until it reaches room temperature.

To make the truffles: The ganache should now be ready for making truffle centers. Scoop the ganache onto parchment paper using a small ice-cream scoop. With the palms of your hands, gently roll the scooped ganache into perfectly round balls. If the ganache is too soft to roll, refrigerate for several minutes.

For the dipping and topping: Now you are ready to dip the truffles. Generously cover the palms of both of your hands with tempered chocolate. (See tempering instructions below.) Pick up a ganache center and roll it in the palms of your hands until it is thoroughly coated. Set on parchment paper; continue until all centers have been coated. When the first coat is hardened, coat your palms with tempered chocolate again and cover truffles with a second coat.

Finish the truffle by sprinkling dried raspberries or placing a small sweet potato curl on the top before the chocolate sets up. The wet chocolate will act as glue, keeping your toppings in place.

Store your truffles at room temperature. They should be enjoyed within 5 days.

How to Temper Chocolate

When you melt chocolate, you take it from its tempered state to its untempered state. So, in order to get the beautiful appearance back, you have to temper it, or "make it behave."

1 pound chocolate, chopped into bite-size pieces

1 microwave-safe bowl

1 rubber spatula

1 digital thermometer

Place ⅔ pound of the chocolate in a microwave-safe bowl. Melt the chocolate, stirring at 30-second intervals, until the chocolate reaches 115°F (110°F if it is white chocolate). Add a small handful of the remaining chocolate bits to the melted chocolate and stir constantly. Repeat this step until all the chocolate has been stirred in and melted or until the chocolate has reached 89°F.

At this point the chocolate should be tempered. You can test it by dipping the end of a plastic utensil into the chocolate and letting it rest for 2 minutes. The chocolate should set up quickly with a shiny finish. When you are tempering chocolate, the temperature of the kitchen should be cool, ideally around 68°F.

CORK & COW

403 Main Street, Franklin
(615) 538-6021
corkandcow.com

Once upon a time, the building at 403 Main Street in Franklin was Jason McConnell's authentic Mexican venture, SOL. This worked very well, but the bellwethers of the local restaurant scene changed, and soon the front bar of SOL and front room permanently morphed into 55 South, and so it remains today. Very recently, Jason opted to turn Sol into a new format, Franklin's first true local steak house. Having been there for the soft opening, I can tell you it was a success from the get-go.

Cork & Cow, with its cork walls and vintage cleavers, clean white tablecloths, and close-set tables, gives you European intimacy with a wholly American attitude. Begin your meal by ordering a cocktail, then the beef carpaccio or warm marinated olives to start. For my money, the New York strip and the rib eye are the way to go, medium rare, because this is truly good beef. Add the triple threat of béarnaise, lump crab, and roasted red peppers, and if you've got an appetite going, perhaps a grilled lobster tail. There are multiple takes on the potato, try the salt-crusted baked potato or the fries with malt vinegar aioli. Order the bacon-wrapped Brussels sprouts on the side (these are marvelous).

Of course, Cork & Cow pairs other sides with their steaks, including pastas, and this one is utterly delicious.

BUTTERNUT ROTOLO

(SERVES 6–8 AS AN APPETIZER OR SIDE DISH)

This is a recipe for an Italian rolled pasta. It takes some time to prep, but it's a great do-ahead dish that will impress.

For the filling:

½ butternut squash

Salt and pepper to taste

1 cup goat cheese

1 cup ricotta cheese

1 tablespoon finely chopped fresh thyme

Pinch of nutmeg

2 cups sautéed spinach

1 tablespoon olive oil

For the pasta:

4 cups flour

6 eggs

For cooking:

1 tablespoon olive oil

For the quick sauce:

2 tablespoons crushed hazelnuts

1 teaspoon finely chopped fresh thyme

Splash of white wine for deglazing

2 or 3 pats cold butter

To make the filling: Preheat oven to 350°F.

Cut the squash in half; reserve one half for another use. Remove the seeds from the remaining half.

Season with salt, pepper, and olive oil. Bake covered for 45 minutes.

Mix the cooked squash together gently with cheeses and spices. Set aside with the spinach.

To make the pasta: Place flour on a cutting board or in a bowl. Make a well in the center and crack eggs into the middle. Whisk eggs with a fork, then with floured hands mix together until incorporated and silky smooth. Cover or wrap with plastic and allow to rest for 30 minutes.

Assembling the rotolo: You should be thinking jelly roll of pasta, so the directions are for spreading, rolling, wrapping with cheesecloth, poaching, and sautéing.

Roll out the pasta with a pasta machine into sheets that are the full width of your machine and approximately 8 inches in length. Spread a layer of the squash mixture, then spread some of the spinach over the top of each sheet of pasta.

Roll each sheet to form a "jelly roll" of filled pasta. Wrap with cheesecloth and tie with butcher's twine on each end.

Bring water to a simmer in a pot that you can fit your wrapped pasta rolls into. Poach the rolls for 10–12 minutes to cook the dough

Remove and chill.

Cooking the rotolo: Remove cheesecloth once the rolls have chilled and cut each roll into pieces that are 2 inches wide. Heat 1 tablespoon olive oil in a sauté pan and sear the rotolo on each side until golden brown, then remove.

Making a quick pan sauce: Once you take the rotolo out of the pan, you can throw in the crushed hazelnuts and chopped thyme, then deglaze with white wine and finish with a few pieces of cold butter. Season with salt and pepper, then pour over the top of rotolo.

CORK & COW COCKTAILS

One of the things Jason McConnell has always excelled at is making sure the cocktail culture of his restaurants defies the ordinary. Both Red Pony and Cork & Cow have intimate bars that you can make into your entire experience. My friend Dena Nance and I have made both the upstairs and downstairs bars at Red Pony our own over the past few years, and now we're learning our way to the luxe black bar in Cork & Cow. The bartenders know us, and on a given evening, we know plenty of the crowd as well.

One of the things that always keeps patrons coming back, you must know, is the effective way both restaurants make use of local and regional distilleries and microdistilleries; here, Corsair Artisan's amazing gin (if you like citrus and juniper, it's for you) and the classic Tennessee whiskey of George Dickel—both recipes from Cork & Cow mixologist Chris Capaldi.

GREEN MEANS GO

1½ ounces Corsair Artisan Gin

¾ ounce Strega

½ ounce basil grapefruit syrup (recipe follows)

½ ounce fresh lime juice

Sprig of fresh rosemary for garnish

Add ingredients to shaker with ice. Shake and strain into ice-filled double old-fashioned glass. Drop rosemary in glass for garnish.

Basil Grapefruit Syrup (makes 16 ounces)

Zest of 2 grapefruits

16 basil leaves

1 cup sugar

1 cup water

Rinse basil and allow it to dry on a towel.

Combine grapefruit zest, fresh basil, sugar, and water in a medium saucepan. Bring to a simmer, stirring occasionally. While stirring, press basil against the saucepan. At first sign of a boil, remove from heat and allow syrup to cool.

Once cooled, strain syrup through a fine-mesh strainer. It will keep refrigerated for up to a month.

CASCADE COOLER

1½ ounces George Dickel Tennessee Whiskey

1 ounce Domaine de Canton

½ ounce Marie Brizard Orange Curacao

½ ounce fresh lemon juice

Thick slice of orange peel for garnish

Add ingredients to shaker with ice. Shake and strain into ice-filled double old-fashioned glass. Gently squeeze orange peel over top of the drink to express oils and drop into drink.

Dozen Bakery

516 Hagan Street, Suite 103, Nashville
(615) 712-8150
dozen-nashville.com

Over the past several years, a collection of independent bakeries have appeared in the area. Perhaps unsurprisingly, most of them work in the cupcake oeuvre; Claire Meneely, however, got us hooked on her cookies, then led us down a path to different things.

Unlike many of those who started when she did, she doesn't have a brick-and-mortar shop. Instead, she does custom orders and private events, and she sells at several farmers' markets, working from her commercial kitchen. I discovered her at the Franklin Farmers' Market, where she quickly got me hooked on ginger and peanut butter cookies. Everything is made with organic, often local, ingredients. You don't often find cookies this incredibly good, at least not here in the US, where we tend toward accepting prepackaged supermarket cookies as the norm.

These days, people line up, phone, and e-mail to order baked goods of every description from Claire, most not realizing the level of training and commitment she has put into her business. She graduated from California Culinary Academy's baking and pastry arts program in 2002, then remained and worked in the San Francisco area, refining her talents. In 2008 she relocated to Paris to study the art of baking under some of the world's masters. She returned to Nashville in 2009, started Dozen, and proceeded to change our sweet palates dramatically for the better.

This is Claire's take on the Southern strawberry shortcake tradition, which can be made year-round to pair with the fruits in season or with fresh jam.

BROWN SUGAR SHORTCAKES
(MAKES 12 2-INCH SHORTCAKES)

1 teaspoon vanilla

1 cup cream

2½ cups flour

¾ cup brown sugar

¾ teaspoon salt

1 tablespoon plus 1 teaspoon baking powder

1 stick (½ cup) unsalted butter, cold and chopped in small pieces

Melted butter, for brushing on top

Sugar, for sprinkling

Preheat oven to 350°F.

Add the vanilla to the cream.

Place the flour, brown sugar, salt, and baking powder in a bowl and whisk to combine.

Using a pastry cutter or rubbing the mixture between your fingers, blend the cold butter into the flour until it resembles coarse meal.

Slowly add cream mixture while stirring until dough just comes together.

Roll out dough 1 inch thick on floured surface. Use a biscuit cutter to cut out shortcakes.*

Brush tops with melted butter, then sprinkle with sugar. Place on a tray and bake for 15 minutes, until golden brown.

Served with homemade whipped cream and seasonal fruit and jams from the farmers' market for a delicious dessert—great with strawberries, grilled peaches, blueberries, stewed apples, or whatever is in season!

*Note: Shortcakes will stand straightest if refrigerated overnight before baking.

FRANKLIN FARMERS MARKET

We're lucky to have an abundance of neighborhood farmers' markets in Nashville, with more sprouting up each year. One of the most longstanding, the Franklin Farmers Market, formed as a 501(c)(5) in 2002 and has flourished into a large Saturday market with a genuine commitment to local growers and their produce. Held in the parking lot and shed behind the Factory at Franklin, the market serves residents of the county and those who drive from surrounding areas.

I live not far from the Franklin Farmers Market, and a large percentage of my husband's and my food dollars is spent here. There are no resellers, plenty of reliable farmers, and there's even a winter market that runs from November to March, ensuring that what's available during Tennessee's long growing season (the past few years, we've gotten fresh tomatoes into November, no hothouse required) reaches the consumer. It's also the spot for many CSA pickups.

Besides produce, we can get local organic meats, eggs, handmade cheeses, breads, honey, plants from area nursery farmers, and non-homogenized milk from grass-fed cows via nearby College Grove, Tennessee's wonderful Hatcher Dairy. With the addition of food vendors, live music, and plenty of local craftspeople during spring, summer, and fall, it's a weekly event everyone in Williamson County who cares about what they're eating doesn't want to miss.

Learn more at franklinfarmersmarket.com.

1808 Grille

1808 West End Avenue (Hutton Hotel), West End
(615) 340-0012
1808grille.com

Set as it is on West End, 1808 Grille is a prime spot for business dining and for travelers, but it's also the kind of place locals frequent for its bold menu and tremendously welcoming atmosphere. The sleek, modern restaurant interior set right off the hotel atrium very much keeps with the vibe of the concept hotel: contemporary elegance at an understated best.

But while lovely, it's still about the power of the menu. The 1808 Burger is a citywide favorite, and the meat and three concept that focuses on three seasonal, local, farm-to-table sides each day, served with your choice of arctic char, flatiron steak, or Ashley's Farm chicken breast, combines the best Southern traditions with the kind of New American style that makes for a seriously popular lunch.

Peaches are a staple in Tennessee in the summer. We even have a peach truck that delivers to neighborhoods. Using them in a delightfully original manner for a pork dish is a no-brainer. This recipe came from former chef Charles Phillips, who never met a peach he didn't want to turn into something magical.

PORK TENDERLOIN WITH PEACH SALAD, SHAVED RADICCHIO & SWEET CHERRY GASTRIQUE

(SERVES 4)

For the pork:

2 pork tenderloins

Marinade or dry rub of your choice

For the peach salad:

4 peaches, cut in half

⅓ cup olive oil

¼ cup small-torn pieces of basil (scissors work well)

¼ cup chopped Italian parsley

½ cup toasted pistachios

Salt and fresh ground pepper to taste

Juice of 1 lemon

1 head radicchio

For the cherry gastrique sauce:

1 cup dried cherries

1 cup frozen cherries

1 cup sherry

½ cup vegetable stock

¼ cup sugar

To prepare the pork: Peel the silver skin off the tenderloins and marinate or use a dry rub. This is space to be creative. You can simply chop some herbs, mix with vegetable oil, and marinate, or use some of your favorite grilling spice. Wrapping the pork in bacon is also an option.

After the pork has marinated for a couple hours, brush off the excess rub or marinade and place it on an outdoor grill at medium heat.

Slow-cook the pork until it is to your liking, but we suggest cooking it to medium well, 160°F internal temperature.

To make the peach salad: Lightly oil the peach halves and give a quick sear on high heat on an outdoor grill or a nonstick pan indoors. The idea is to caramelize a bit of the natural sugar without cooking the peach. It must remain crisp, not turn mushy.

Cut the peach half in half again. Toss the peaches with the herbs, oil, pistachio, salt, pepper, and lemon juice to taste. Slice the radicchio very thin and toss everything together.

To make the cherry gastrique sauce: Combine all the listed ingredients in a sauce pot and reduce to a syrup consistency. Place in a blender and puree until very smooth.

To serve: With a pastry brush, "paint" a heavy line of cherry gastrique sauce across the plate. Place a small amount of the peach salad in the center of the plate. Slice the pork into 1-inch medallions and place 3 slices on top of the salad. (Allow pork to rest a few minutes before cutting.)

THE COCKTAILS

May in Tennessee means horse racing season. Not only are we horse country, but beyond the usual first weekend Kentucky Derby, we have our own tradition: The second Saturday in May, we head out to the Iroquois Steeplechase in Belle Meade, named in honor of the great champion of the local Belle Meade line.

With that in mind, lest you think all juleps are out of Kentucky, here are two variations on a classic racing cocktail made with Tennessee whiskey.

TENNESSEE JULEP

½ ounce simple syrup

Small handful of fresh mint leaves

1½ ounces Prichard's Sweet Lucy Liqueur

Soda water

Make the simple syrup by mixing 2 parts sugar with 1 part water. Bring the water to a boil, add sugar, and dissolve, stirring constantly. Allow to cool and store extra in a squeeze bottle in the refrigerator for easy use.

Muddle mint leaves and simple syrup in an empty double old-fashioned glass. Add ice and Sweet Lucy Liqueur. Finish with a splash of soda.

Prefer a sweeter cocktail? Before serving, rim the glass with sugar.

WEST END JULEP

Small handful of fresh mint leaves

1 ounce Bitter Truth Apricot Liqueur

2 ounces Prichard's Tennessee Whiskey

Soda water

Muddle mint and Bitter Truth Apricot Liqueur in an empty highball glass. Add ice and Prichard's whiskey. Finish with a splash of soda.

Find Prichard's products through your local distributor; for more information visit prichardsdistillery .com.

8TH AND ROAST

2108 8th Avenue South, Antiques District
(615) 730-8074
4104 Charlotte Avenue, Sylvan Station
(615) 988-4020
Nashville International Airport
8thandroast.com

Coffee culture in Nashville has often seemed heavily focused in East Nashville, Hillsboro/Belmont, or over in the 12South neighborhood, but the 2012 move and expansion of Roast, Inc., brought one of the best and most dedicated coffee companies to 8th Avenue South and the Antiques District—and brought better-than-fair-trade coffees that are truly excellent, whether you want a cup of black or something with a few more ingredients. What they do is coffee, and they do it right.

8th and Roast has changed hands since Lesa Wood originally opened on 8th Avenue South a few years ago, but they remain committed to high quality coffee drinks and the accompanying treats, such as the muffin recipe that follows. Set in a nearly-century-old building with reclaimed-bowling-alley-wood tables and vintage light fixtures, it's one of my favorite atmospheres, especially on dark, wintery afternoons. The vibe on 8th Avenue South, just south of the bustling Gulch and just north of the funky Berry Hill always feels warm and welcoming to me. Antiques stores, a comedy club, and older neighborhoods nearby add to that. When you just need a break in the shopping, driving, or work day—8th and Roast remains a place for solace with a distinct vintage energy. There are two other locations: one on Charlotte Avenue and the other at the Nashville International Airport.

DIRTY CHAI MUFFINS

3½ cups all-purpose flour

1 tablespoon baking power

1 teaspoon salt

1 teaspoon each: cinnamon, ginger, ground cloves

5 ounces melted butter (about 1¼ sticks)

1½ cups sugar

2 eggs

2 teaspoons vanilla extract

1 cup cooled coffee

2½ cups powdered sugar

¼ cup espresso

Espresso powder for dusting (optional)

Mix flour, baking powder, salt, and spices together in a mixing bowl.

Whisk together butter, sugar, and eggs in a separate bowl. Fold the wet ingredients into the dry until thoroughly blended. Bake in a lightly greased muffin tin at 350°F for 20 minutes.

Whisk together powdered sugar and espresso powder until blended. Apply to muffins when they have cooled.

Optionally top the muffin with espresso powder.

ETCH

303 Demonbreun Street, Downtown
(615) 522-0685
etchrestaurant.com

Chef Deb Paquette is nothing short of a Nashville legend—a graduate of the Culinary Institute of America, she's best known for the many years she and husband Ernie spent as owners of Zola restaurant, winning national and local awards for the incredible fare Deb magically brought to life. When Zola closed, the city collectively mourned as Chef Deb and Ernie took off for the Caribbean before the owners of a popular Italian restaurant wooed them back with an offer Deb couldn't refuse.

In short, they gave her the opportunity to create a signature restaurant in the Encore building. While the build-out happened, Deb served as consultant to 12South's Urban Grub restaurant and helped Jeff and Jenny Pennington develop their exquisite microdistillery product, Whisper Creek. Adding to her fine reputation as a consultant, everything she touched developed significant buzz and made the excitement for Etch even stronger.

In 2012 Etch came beautifully together, on the ground floor of the Encore tower. The space provides a private dining room, bar, and an open kitchen with bar-style seating so you can interact directly with the chef and her kitchen (and she's a joy to watch—they all are).

The menu is creative and diverse, changing seasonally. A sampling of Deb's menu might have you contemplating starters like Chinese braised pork or octopus and shrimp bruschetta; the Etch Salad offers up fennel, green apple, arugula, radicchio, blue cheese, hazelnuts, and a champagne vinaigrette. For an entree, you might consider the pork tenderloin or the Moroccan spiced venison.

The following recipe can be used for that spiced venison as well as for duck breast, depending on your preference. "This dish has many components," Deb tells me, "but all very easy and fun."

ETCH DUCK BREAST WITH GINGER GRITS, SWEET POTATO GUAVA SCHMEAR, CRANBERRY RELISH & PEAR BUTTER

(SERVES 6-8)

Venison may easily be substituted for duck in this recipe. Where noted, some of these steps can be done a day in advance for ease of preparation. The spice is called *Ras el hanout,* which, according to Deb, means "head of the shop" or "don't touch your mama's spice."

DUCK BREAST OR VENISON:

4 large duck moulard (double breasts) or one per person if using small breasts or 1½ pounds venison

1 tablespoon cumin seed

1 tablespoon fennel seed

2 tablespoons coriander seed

1 teaspoon ground ginger

1 teaspoon cinnamon

1 teaspoon black pepper

1 teaspoon turmeric

¼ teaspoon nutmeg

¼ teaspoon ground clove

¼ teaspoon allspice

1 teaspoon cayenne

1 teaspoon cardamom

2 tablespoons sugar

1 tablespoon kosher salt

Grind seeds to a fine powder. Mix all the seeds and spices together well and store in a jar.

If there is a lot of fat on the duck, remove a layer to not have more than ¼ inch. Score fat, being careful not to cut the meat. Place breast fat-side down on a metal pan and freeze until fat is firm. Lightly salt breast and sear fat-side down in a low-heated sauté pan to help render fat. (Do not brown.) Cool and put in fridge. A half hour before grilling, season generously with the spice mixture and let sit at room temperature. Grill carefully to avoid burning your spices and reach a nice medium-rare temperature. Let sit 10 minutes before slicing.

GINGER GRITS

1 quart water

1 stick (½ cup) butter

1 teaspoon salt

1 teaspoon black pepper

1¾ cups stone-ground grits

½ cup candied ginger (choose the syrupy type)

Fresh grated ginger to taste, if desired

Boil water with butter, salt, and black pepper. Stir in grits with a whisk. Cook on low heat until thick, about 20 minutes. If too thick, add a bit of water. If too thin, add a touch more grits.

When grits no longer have their rawness, add candied ginger. If you want more sweetness and ginger flavor, add a bit more candied ginger, or add fresh grated for more of a bite.

Hold warm until ready to serve.

SWEET POTATO GUAVA SCHMEAR

2 pounds sweet potatoes

2–3 ounces guava paste

4–6 tablespoons unsalted butter

Pinch of salt

Roast the sweet potatoes at 350°F until soft, about ½ hour; or poke with a fork to vent then microwave 10 minutes, turning after 5 minutes.

Peel the potatoes when warm and place in a food processor with guava paste and butter. Puree until it reaches a baby food consistency. Add a pinch of salt.

This can be made ahead of time and reheated in the microwave or served room temperature.

CRANBERRY RELISH

(MAKES 12 OUNCES)

3 cups frozen cranberries

½ cup sugar

1 tablespoon sumac (found at Middle Eastern grocery stores or international markets)

Juice and zest of 1 lime

½ teaspoon salt

1 serrano pepper, seeds removed and chopped

½ cup walnut oil

½ teaspoon toasted cumin seeds, ground

½ bunch cilantro, chopped

Place all the ingredients except the cilantro in a food processor. Pulse until berries are broken up into bits. Do not puree. Add chopped cilantro.

This can be made a day in advance. Leftovers are wonderful on toast or sweet potatoes.

PEAR BUTTER

(MAKES 16 OUNCES)

4 sticks (2 cups) butter

½ cup pear liqueur (Mathilde preferred)

½ cup pear puree

½ teaspoon cayenne

Pinch of salt

2 tablespoons sugar

Dice up the butter and put in a mixer. Slowly begin to whip the butter, then slowly add pear liqueur and pear puree and allow to emulsify. Add cayenne, salt, and sugar and whip till fluffy.

Put in an airtight container and refrigerate until needed, but pull out in time to soften a bit before serving. (Save extra for your morning bagel!)

BANANA FUN DOTS

1 ripe banana

½ teaspoon turmeric

1 teaspoon sugar

¼ cup walnut oil

¼ cup water

Place all the ingredients in a blender and puree till smooth. Transfer to a squirt bottle.

Plating the dish: Put a nice big schmear of sweet potato puree on the plate. Place a scoop of grits on the schmear. Place sliced grilled duck around the grits. Add 2 teaspoons pear butter to grits, flowing onto duck, or set it on the table and let guests plop it on themselves. Add about 1 tablespoon cranberry relish to the side of the grits. Squirt banana dots around the plate to garnish. Some nice greens poking out of the grits is a fabulous touch.

TUNA, EGGPLANT & SPINACH PONZU SALAD

(SERVES 4–6)

Zola, Chef Deb Paquette's previous restaurant, which she closed a few years ago after thirteen years at the top of Nashville's dining scene, had a reputation for outstanding salads. Her new location, Etch, is building a similar reputation, in part due to the original thinking of Sous Chef Kenji Nakagawa. Like other recipes Paquette contributed to this book, this one is a multistep process, but many pieces can be created in advance, and none of them are terribly complicated. The real priority is getting the right ingredients, like Chinese or Japanese eggplant and really good tuna from your fishmonger.

For the marinated eggplant:

3 pounds Chinese or Japanese eggplant

Canola or peanut oil for frying

10 ounces citrus vinegar

1¼ cups soy sauce

½ cup rice vinegar

½ cup sugar

2 ounces water

1 ounce mushroom soy sauce

1 ounce oyster sauce

1 teaspoon minced ginger

For the ponzu vinaigrette:

(Make in advance and put in fridge to allow flavors to develop.)

6 ounces citrus seasoning (available at Asian markets)

5 ounces soy sauce

3 ounces rice vinegar

3 tablespoons sugar

2 ounces sake

1½ ounces water

½ teaspoon Coleman's mustard

1 tablespoon lemon juice

1 tablespoon lime juice

2 teaspoons fresh ginger

1 cup canola oil

¼ cup sesame oil

For the spiced tuna:

1 tablespoon red pepper flakes

¼ cup fennel seed

3 tablespoons paprika

2 tablespoons salt

12–18 ounces quality tuna (2–3 ounces per person)

1 tablespoon sesame oil for coating tuna

For the salad:

½ cup daikon, cut in small pieces

1 brick smoked tofu, cut in small pieces

3 ounces button mushrooms, thinly sliced

5 spring onions, sliced on the bias

About 2 pounds fresh spinach (5–6 ounces per person)

Optional additions: cilantro, broccoli, sprouts

Red bell pepper slivers for garnish

To prepare the eggplant: Cut the stems off and cut the eggplant into quarters. Cut each quarter into 3- to 4-inch pieces.

Use a fryer or heat 2 inches of oil in a wide pot or skillet. Bring the oil temperature to 350°F. Meanwhile, place a 2-quart pot of water on the stove and bring to a boil.

Deep-fry the eggplant for 30–45 seconds until it turns bright purple and softens (you may need to do this in batches). Drain well. When all is fried, place the eggplant into boiling water for 10 seconds. Shock it in ice water and drain. Place a towel on a sheet pan and set eggplant to dry. Let dry for 1 hour before placing in marinade.

Mix the marinade ingredients (citrus vinegar, soy sauce, rice vinegar, sugar, water, mushroom soy sauce, oyster sauce, and minced ginger) in a bowl and whisk to blend. Pour over the eggplant in a shallow dish. Place a plate on top to hold the eggplant down in the marinade. Marinate for at least 2 hours; overnight is fine. The marinade is good for 3–4 days.

To make the vinaigrette: Blend all the ingredients at high speed in a blender for 1 minute. It will look foamy at first, but will quickly settle down.

To prepare the tuna: Grind the red pepper flakes, fennel seed, and paprika. Place in a bowl, add the salt, and mix well.

Cut the tuna into 6- x 3-inch pieces. Slather with a light coating of sesame oil, then generously coat tuna with spice mix. Add the spice to the fish, not the fish to the bowl, so you don't contaminate the spice mix if you have extra.

Set your sauté pan on medium heat with oil covering the bottom of the pan. Heat each side of the tuna so all sides get ⅛–¼ inch of cooking. Cool the tuna, then refrigerate to rest for at least 1 hour.

To prepare the salad: Toss all the salad ingredients with 3–4 ounces of ponzu vinaigrette (shake well first).

To assemble: Plate salad onto individual plates and top with thin, chilled slices of the tuna and eggplant. Toss red bell pepper for color.

FLOURLESS CHOCOLATE CAKE WITH
COFFEE CRÈME BRÛLÉE, MILK CHOCOLATE CRUMBLE & MOCHA MOUSSE

There are few desserts on the Etch menu that limit themselves to a single flavor component—instead, when you visit, expect layered flavors that make your mouth celebrate the combinations. The flourless aspect of this particular recipe makes it a good selection for those on a gluten-free diet. But like most true gastronomic dessert delights, the calorie count might mean a few extra crunches in the morning for the health conscious—because skipping it isn't an option. (Note: It's best to use a reliable food scale for this recipe.)

(SERVES 8-10)

For the chocolate cake:

8 ounces (1 cup) dark chocolate (55% cocoa solids or higher)

3 ounces (6 tablespoons) butter

Pinch of salt

½ teaspoon vanilla extract

2 eggs

1 egg yolk

1 tablespoon sugar

For the coffee crème brûlée:

1 ounce (2 tablespoons) coffee

10 ounces (1 cup plus 2 tablespoons) cream

1½ ounces (3 tablespoons) sugar

1½ sheets gelatin, bloomed

3 egg yolks

1 teaspoon espresso powder

For the milk chocolate crumble:

4½ ounces (1 tablespoon) milk powder, divided

3 ounces (¼ cup plus 2 tablespoons) cocoa powder

½ ounce (1 tablespoon) cornstarch

2 ounces (¼ cup) rice flour

2 ounces (¼ cup) sugar

½ ounce (1 tablespoon) salt

4 ounces (½ cup) butter, melted

5 ounces (½ cup plus 2 tablespoons) milk chocolate, melted

For the mocha mousse:

2 tablespoons water

2½ ounces (¼ cup plus 1 tablespoon) sugar

21½ ounces cream, divided (5½ ounces hot)

6 egg yolks

1½ sheets gelatin, bloomed

9 ounces (1 cup plus 2 tablespoons) dark chocolate (55% cocoa solids or higher)

¼ teaspoon salt

2 teaspoons coffee extract

To make the cake: Preheat oven to 300°F for convection, 325°F for conventional.

Melt chocolate and butter in a double boiler. Remove from heat and whisk in salt and vanilla.

In a mixer with a whisk attachment, whip eggs and sugar to a thick ribbon. Fold egg mixture into chocolate mixture in thirds.

Spray a 7- or 8-inch cake pan with cooking spray, line with a parchment circle, and spread batter in pan. Bake for about 10 minutes, until cake is set but slightly jiggly in the center.

To make the crème brûlée: Roast coffee grounds in oven on 300°F in a small baking pan or cake pan until it smells slightly burned.

Heat cream to a simmer in a 1- to 2-quart sauce pan, add toasted coffee, and whisk to combine. Remove from heat, cover, and let steep for 1 hour.

Strain out coffee grounds with a mesh strainer. Add sugar and bring to a simmer in a fresh pan, if possible. Whisk in gelatin.

Temper cream into yolks slowly, then add espresso powder. Strain mixture.

Spray a 7- or 8-inch cake pan with cooking spray, line with plastic wrap, and then pour in the crème brûlée mixture. Freeze.

To make the crumble: Combine 3 ounces milk powder, cocoa powder, cornstarch, rice flour, sugar, and salt in a medium-size bowl. Add melted butter and mix by hand to form small clusters.

Spread on parchment and bake at 200°F in a convection oven, 225°F in a conventional oven, for 20 minutes.

Cool completely. Add remaining 1½ ounces milk powder and toss. Pour in milk chocolate and toss to coat all clusters. Continue to toss every 5 minutes until the chocolate hardens and the clusters are no longer sticky. Refrigerate.

To make the mousse: Caramelize the sugar by adding the water to a small saucepan (about 1-quart size), then add the sugar. Cook over medium-high heat until the sugar cooks to a medium amber color.

Then slowly add 5 ½ ounces hot cream, keeping on medium heat until the mixture boils and the caramel melts into the cream.

Temper the mixture into the egg yolks (stir a little hot cream mixture into the yolks to raise their temperature), then pour the tempered yolks back into the pot with the rest of the hot cream mixture, and cook over very low heat for about 1 minute, stirring constantly with a wooden spoon or heat proof spatula. (You are essentially making a crème anglaise.)

Add gelatin, whisk to melt, and then strain over chocolate, salt, and coffee extract. Whisk to combine and make a ganache. Whip the remaining 16 ounces cream to very soft peaks and fold into chocolate mixture in thirds.

To assemble: Line the bottom of a 9- or 10-inch springform pan with parchment. Put the flourless cake in the pan and then a crème brûlée layer in the center. Add half of the mousse, spread, and whack on counter to get air bubbles out. Sprinkle about 1½ cups of milk chocolate crumble over the mousse layer. Eat the rest as a snack. Pour on remainder of mousse. Spread top smooth and freeze overnight. Defrost for 2 hours in the refrigerator before slicing.

WHISPER CREEK WAKEUP CHILLER

(SERVES 4)

Deb Paquette is a master chef, but also pretty incredible when it comes to whipping up flavors for a cocktail. That's why Jeff and Jenny Pennington came to her when they wanted to flavor their Whisper Creek Tennessee Sipping Cream—a beverage not unlike "Irish" cream liqueurs, but made entirely with whiskey (made by local distiller Collier & McKeel), instead of vodka with a little whiskey, for flavor. Working with the Penningtons, Deb helped define the beverage's flavors fully, not only the cream, but the natural notes of whiskey—caramel, burnt molasses, fig, red apple, and pecan. If you don't have access to Whisper Creek, you can use your favorite cream liqueur, but with its growing national availability, we really recommend it. If Whisper Creek is not available where you live, visit tennesseesipping cream.com to order.

2 medium-ripe bananas (not too green)

2 cups ice

½ cup Whisper Creek Tennessee Sipping Cream

1 tablespoon freeze-dried coffee or 1 teaspoon coffee extract

1 tablespoon peeled and minced fresh ginger

1 cup half-and-half (substitute milk if you want to cut calories)

Place all the ingredients in a blender and blend well. The recipe makes enough for 4 good servings to rejuvenate your brain. Remember, you have some banana for potassium, caffeine to stimulate, ginger to balance the belly, calcium for your bones, water to hydrate, and Whisper Creek to soothe the soul (if in doubt, add more Whisper Creek).

FIDO

1812 21st Avenue South, Hillsboro Village
(615) 777-3436
fidocafe.com

FIDO has been around for more than a decade now, one of several cafes under the umbrella of owner and coffee roaster Bob Bernstein. We might have come late to the coffee revolution as a city—only in the past few years has the locally roasted coffee thing really exploded—but Bob has been on this path since at least 1993, when he opened Bongo Java, his first cafe and roasting house offering fair trade or better coffees roasted right here (why, yes, you can buy it online). A commitment to sustainability means FIDO, which is as much restaurant as coffee business for Bernstein, makes use of plenty of local and organic foods where they can.

FIDO is usually filled with Vanderbilt or Belmont students, along with businesspeople taking a break and advantage of the Wi-Fi as well as slurping down excellent coffee. There's a fine menu of salads, sandwiches, omelets (breakfast served all day), and more. The baked goods in the glass case as you wait in line to order are completely irresistible, from homemade cookies to rich chocolate zucchini cake.

The pumpkin chocolate-chip muffins here are more than worth the effort if you want to really impress your guests.

THE PC MUFFIN

(MAKES 10 LARGE MUFFINS)

½ cup sugar

½ cup packed brown sugar

½ cup canola oil

½ cup olive oil

½ cup unsweetened applesauce

1¾ cups canned pumpkin

3 eggs

3½ cups flour

2 teaspoons cinnamon

1 teaspoon cloves

1 teaspoon nutmeg

1½ teaspoons baking soda

1½ teaspoons baking powder

1 teaspoon salt

1½ cups chocolate chips

Preheat oven to 275°F.

Combine the sugars, oils, applesauce, pumpkin, and eggs in a mixer with a paddle attachment on the middle speed or whisk by hand at a rapid rate until all the ingredients are evenly mixed.

In a separate bowl, combine the remaining dry ingredients. Turn the mixer off and add dry ingredients to the wet ingredients. Blend on a low speed or by hand with a whisk until evenly mixed.

Spray a muffin tin with Baker's Joy or use muffin papers. Use a spoon to place approximately ¾ cup of batter into each muffin cup. Bake for about 30 minutes, rotating the pan after 15 minutes.

Use a toothpick to check the muffins. If the toothpick comes out clean, the muffins are done; if it has batter stuck to it, the muffins need about 5 more minutes.

55 SOUTH

403 Main Street, Franklin
(615) 538-6001
7031 Executive Drive, Brentwood
(615) 610-3382
eat55south.com

My husband and I have spent many a Sunday morning at 55 South, partaking of brunch. Let me just say that the French toast (Pecan Pain Perdu) here is among the best—and one of my personal comfort foods. Of course, there's plenty on the brunch menu to love, including the Fried Pork Chop Sandwich with avocado and hot sauce, the NOLA Omelet, or maybe the 55 Wedge with blue cheese dressing (pretty classic Nashville, the iceberg wedge salad).

The bar is a regular draw, not just for Sunday Bloody Marys, but after work on a weekday, when the whole of Franklin converges to shoot oysters, visit with friends, and sip on the happy hour specials.

Folks love 55 South for oysters and whiskey (including the distilleries of Tennessee and Kentucky). The menu concept showcases the cuisine you find when you drive I-55 south from Memphis down to New Orleans, with a little Nashville for good measure. From the pork chop mentioned earlier to gumbo and jambalaya, there's a little Tennessee, a little Mississippi, a bit of Louisiana—there's even a hint of Mexico, including handmade guacamole.

The recipe for Nashville Hot Chicken is Chef Jason's take on pure Nashville, the hot chicken phenomenon (find another take, from Biscuit Love Truck, on page 21). Jason's variation combines a hot rub that will tingle your taste buds (or more, if you up the cayenne content) but that mediates the heat with the classic tang of mayo and the simplicity of white bread—just the way you might with a spicy barbecue sauce (where the mayo would come with the coleslaw).

NASHVILLE HOT CHICKEN

(SERVES 6)

As 55 South recommends, these sandwiches pair perfectly with coleslaw and potato chips.

For the paste and chicken:

1 tablespoon cayenne pepper

1 tablespoon paprika

2 tablespoons garlic powder

1 teaspoon salt

1 teaspoon black pepper

1½ tablespoons Louisiana Hot Sauce
   (or a similar brand)

3 tablespoons vegetable oil

¼ cup water

6 (6-ounce) chicken breasts, boneless and skinless

2 cups flour, preseasoned with salt and pepper

Oil for frying

For the sandwiches:

12 slices white bread

1 cup mayo

Nashville Hot Chicken Paste

6 kosher pickles, sliced, or to taste

To marinate the chicken: Make the Nashville Hot Chicken Paste by combining the spices, hot sauce, vegetable oil, and water in a bowl. Rub the chicken with half the paste. Reserve the rest for spreading on the finished sandwich. Refrigerate the chicken and the remaining paste overnight.

To prepare the chicken: Dredge the marinated chicken breast in seasoned flour, and place in a deep fryer at 350°F. Cook for 3 minutes or until chicken is floating at the top of the oil. If you are using a pan

instead of a deep fryer, your cooking oil needs to be about an inch deep. Fry the chicken pieces to a deep brown (at least 1½–2 minutes) on each side.

To assemble the sandwiches: Spread mayo on all the slices of bread, and place a cooked chicken breast on half of them. Drizzle with the Nashville Hot Chicken Paste, then top with pickle slices and the second piece of bread. Cut sandwiches in half and serve.

HOT CHICKEN

There exist any number of "Southern"—or at least Southern by association—foods you find repeated again and again on menus south of the Mason-Dixon. Increasingly, you'll find takes on things you never saw before in Brooklyn, Los Angeles, or Seattle, as Southern foodways trends take hold.

That being the case, it's hard to say where many of these foods originated definitively—shrimp and grits, sure, they used to be Low Country, but they're everywhere now. Pecan pie, corn bread . . . the list goes on. Memphis, Charleston, New Orleans, they all have signature dishes. But Nashville? Well, for us, it's probably hot chicken.

By hot, I mean spicy. I mean break-a-sweat-on-the-second-bite spicy.

The first true Nashville hot chicken is reputed to have been created by the girlfriend of one Thornton Prince more than sixty years ago. He had a reputation as a ladies' man, and his significant other didn't like that one bit. After he spent a memorable night chasing skirts, the girlfriend in question fixed him some hellaciously spicy fried chicken as fiery vengeance. He liked it so much, he started serving it in his restaurant.

Thornton's niece, Andre Prince, has been the proprietor of Prince's Hot Chicken Shack (123 Ewing Drive) since 1980. Line up and order mild, medium, hot, or extra hot (really, start with mild, it will still burn). All sandwiches come with white bread and pickles to (ha!) mediate the heat.

Over the years a number of restaurants have taken hot chicken very seriously. I'm a big fan of Pepperfire (2821 Gallatin Road), among others. Even country stars Lorrie Morgan and Sammy Kers once had their own restaurant. It's gotten to be so popular that we've created a Hot Chicken Festival (mchcf.blogspot.com) in recent years. Big Shake's Chicken and Fish, which started in a back corner of Franklin and now has a prime spot in Williamson County at the corner of Highway 96 and Royal Oaks in Cool Springs, has gained some serious fandom—rightfully—in the past year or two. I'm not going to lie—it's close to my office, and I'm a regular patron.

I've included two really good hot chicken recipes in this book for you to try: One is from 55 South, and while pretty spicy, you needn't fear singeing the lips of dinner guests—and it's definitely still comfort food. The second comes from one of the best food trucks around, Biscuit Love. The Princess Biscuit, named in tribute to America's Classics James Beard Award–winning Prince's, adds honey and stone-ground mustard to balance the heat and define the flavors.

FirePOT NOMADIC TeaS

2905 12th Avenue South, Suite 106, 12South
facebook.com/firepot-chai

While coffee seems to be blooming in the South, tea still stands as a little more exotic. Not that we don't have tons of sweet tea around here but, heavens, we make that with tea bags from Lipton and Luzianne. The pleasure of true blended tea is something else entirely. Firepot Nomadic Teas makes that difference come alive for us.

When Sarah Scarborough began her tea odyssey, her first creation was an amazing chai blend she called Firepot Chai. Rich, deeply spiced, and flavorful, the blend became a huge hit with friends and family and built a longtime customer following.

That continued even as Scarborough went out and created a wide variety of products for other companies, traveling the world from New Zealand to China, she learned the ins and outs of the tea world and tea markets. At the time, her goal was producing organic, fair trade and better artisan teas. Now she's returned and settled in Nashville, leaving the corporate tea world behind to focus on the lush chai blend that started it all.

In August 2013 she opened this artisan tea microbrewery in 12South, between Sloco and Burger Up, in one of the city's most in-demand pieces of culinary real estate. Here you'll find Sarah grinding, blending, and brewing teas.

Likewise, instead of offering up Southern sweet tea to pair with the recipes here, let's try a couple of cocktails and even a marinade made with Sarah's international award-winning chai. You can order her incredible chai concentrate directly at firepot.com. Trust me, you'll drink the concentrate all by itself if you're a tea lover. Being one myself, I can attest to this.

CHAI FRIED CHICKEN

(SERVES 4)

The chicken needs to marinate for two nights, but the end result is truly worth the wait! Serve alongside a salad dressed with Firepot Chai Salad Dressing/Marinade (recipe below).

4 chicken breasts or 6 chicken thighs

1 bottle dill pickle juice, pickles removed

5 teaspoons loose-leaf Firepot Black Tea Chai,* divided

2 cups buttermilk

2 cups flour

3 teaspoons baking powder

1 teaspoon salt

Oil for frying

Cover the chicken with pickle juice and soak overnight.

Drain and rinse the chicken. Set aside.

Steep 4 teaspoons of Firepot Black Tea Chai in 2 cups of boiling water for 5 minutes. Strain and cool the chai.

Combine steeped tea with buttermilk. Add chicken and refrigerate for 8 hours or overnight.

Combine flour, 1 teaspoon of Firepot Black Tea Chai, baking powder, and salt. Fill a cast-iron skillet with 1 inch of canola oil. Heat to medium.

Dredge the chicken in the flour mixture and fry in the skillet for about 8 minutes on each side, until done.

*Note: Order Firepot Black Tea Chai from FirePot.com

FIREPOT CHAI SALAD DRESSING/MARINADE
(MAKES 12 OUNCES)

This marinade works for far more than fried chicken, I like it on pork loin, and if you're a fan of salads topped with meat, use it as a delicious dressing on your greens, or marinate your chicken or salmon in it prior to grilling. The tea and citrus combination pairs beautifully with salmon.

2 teaspoons Firepot Black Tea Chai steeped in
½ cup boiling water for 5 minutes

1 cup cold-pressed olive oil

¼ cup apple cider vinegar

2 tablespoons freshly squeezed orange juice

1 tablespoon freshly squeezed lemon juice

1 tablespoon tamari

Combine ingredients in a jar. Cover and chill. Keep refrigerated for up to 1 week.

THE CAUVERI COCKTAIL

Truly, bourbon is a Kentucky thing, and whiskey is a Tennessee thing, but we're all for cultural exchanges (and Nashville is so close to the state line). You get a bit of sweetness here from the chai concentrate, a citrus kick from the lime, and added depth from the bitters—it's a terrific alternative to the old-school julep.

2 ounces Kentucky bourbon

1 tablespoon fresh lime juice

1 tablespoon plus 1 teaspoon Firepot
Chai Concentrate

3 dashes orange bitters

4 ounces soda water

Combine all the ingredients in a glass filled with ice.

FIREPOT CHAI HOT TODDY

It does get cold outside here, and I suspect this cocktail will perk you up if you've got a bit of a cold, too. Bourbon, honey, and water are old Southern prescriptions for sniffles and scratchy throats, but the chai syrup makes that blend taste like Christmas, with its rich spices.

1 ounce Kentucky bourbon

1 tablespoon lemon juice

1 tablespoon Firepot Chai Concentrate

1 teaspoon honey

4 ounces hot water

Combine all the ingredients in a mug and stir until blended.

FLYTE WORLD DINING AND WINE

718 Division Street, 8th Avenue South, The Gulch
(615) 255-6200
flytenashville.com

Flyte World Dining and Wine rests at the far edge of The Gulch, across the street from Arnold's, next door to one of the city's favorite wine and liquor emporiums, just before you hit the Convention Center along 8th Avenue South. When Scott Sears and Scott Atkinson opened the restaurant in 2007, the almost immediate recession meant restaurants closing left and right. Flyte, with its signature flytes of extraordinary wine, tapas in the bar, and marvelous inventive menu, proved a powerhouse survivor.

This dish may seem on the exotic side, but it's delicious, as Flyte patrons know. It plays on the notion of chicken and waffles and the traditional bacon and waffles and creates something distinct. It's the creation of former chef Matt Lackey, and to me this is a complete delight.

It's served with a buttermilk panna cotta, but that isn't practical for a home cook, so they've given you buttermilk dressing recipe to pair with it. The pig ears have a chewy porkiness, without bacon's smoky flavor.

PIG EARS WITH WAFFLES

(SERVES 6-8)

A scale is critical to achieve correct proportions for the waffles.

For the yeasted waffles:

340 grams whole milk (Flyte sources from Hatcher Dairy, a local non-homogenized source.)

4 grams sugar

7 grams instant yeast

84 grams butter (82% fat)

2 farm eggs

50 grams grade A maple syrup

240 grams White Lily all-purpose flour

3 grams salt

For the buttermilk dressing:

160 grams buttermilk (Flyte sources from local Cruz Family Dairy.)

72 grams crème fraîche

44 grams mayonnaise (Duke's preferred)

6 grams togarashi (a Japanese hot pepper staple available at Asian grocery stores and in some supermarkets in the ethnic foods section)

1½ grams salt

1 gram black pepper

For the pig ears:

500 grams pig ears (available from your butcher)

250 grams pork stock

2 grams salt

10 grams Tabasco or your favorite hot sauce

To make the waffles: Heat milk to 106°F (using a thermometer), then add the sugar and remove from heat. Add the instant yeast and allow this yeast starter to rest for 20 minutes.

Melt the butter.

Lightly fold the eggs, maple syrup, and flour together until they are incorporated. Then fold in the yeast starter from above.

Finish by lightly folding in the salt. Cover the bowl with plastic wrap and allow it to rest for 2 hours.

Spoon the batter into your hot waffle iron, until it just lightly covers the skillet. Cook all the batter and reserve the waffles in a warm oven until ready to serve.

To make the dressing: Thoroughly whisk all the ingredients together in a bowl. Refrigerate while the waffles cook.

To prepare the pig ears: Place all the ingredients except hot sauce in a pressure cooker set to high and cook for 50 minutes.

When finished, release pressure and lay the ears out in a single layer. Allow them to cool, then cut the ears into ½-inch strips.

Fry the ears at 360°F until they are golden brown. Toss in a bowl with your favorite hot sauce.

To assemble the dish: Set some pig ears atop a waffle on a plate, and drizzle with buttermilk dressing.

THE GRILLED CHEESERIE GOURMET GRILLED CHEESE TRUCK

2003 Belcourt Avenue, Nashville
(615) 203-0351

One of the favorite food trucks to arrive on the scene in recent years is the Grilled Cheeserie. Working on the theory that there's really nothing as soothing and comfort-inducing as a really good grilled cheese sandwich, Crystal De Luna-Bogan has turned that sandwich into something of an art form. Now, wherever the truck parks, you'll see lines forming and smiles on faces. (I'm lucky, because they cater for my office at least once every six weeks or so.)

The concept works in part because Crystal uses artisan products, among them Sweetwater Valley cheddar from East Tennessee (you can buy it online at sweetwatervalley.com) and fresh bread made by Silke's Old World Breads, a local baker (this too can be ordered, at silkesoldworld breads.com). The addition of Benton's Bacon, another Tennessee artisan icon, really just makes for perfection.

If you prefer to buy local, Crystal says you can absolutely find artisan breads and cheeses in your own region. But the secret to a really delicious sandwich is taking that step from pre-packaged, processed cheese and bread from the local mega-mart and moving toward food made fresh and perfectly from artisan sources. You'll support your small business owners and in the process get something tantalizing and delicious.

Along with the sandwich comes the Grilled Cheeserie's apple and onion jam, which makes this the most brilliant comfort food you've ever tasted. This is heaven. Now serve it up with the tomato soup recipe here and every rainy day will fly by unnoticed.

GRILLED CHEESE

(MAKES 8 SANDWICHES)

1 cup butter, softened

1 loaf Silke's Seeded Multigrain Bread (or your local artisan multigrain)

8–10 slices Sweetwater Valley Buttermilk Cheddar (or your local artisan cheddar)

1 cup (more if desired) Caramelized Apple & Onion Jam (recipe follows)

16–20 slices Benton's Bacon (or other smoky bacon of your choice), baked in 350°F oven on a sheet tray for 15–20 minutes

Preheat a skillet over medium heat.

For each sandwich, generously butter both sides of a slice of multigrain bread. Place bread onto skillet and add a slice of cheese. Top with desired amount of apple and onion jam and 2–3 slices bacon. Butter a second slice of bread on both sides and place on top of sandwich.

Grill until lightly browned and flip over; continue grilling until cheese is melted. Repeat with remaining bread and cheese to complete your sandwiches.

Follow us on Twitter
@grlldcheeserie

CARAMELIZED APPLE & ONION JAM

(MAKES ABOUT 1 CUP, ENOUGH FOR 4-6 SANDWICHES)

2 tablespoons butter, divided

2 large onions, small diced

1 cup unfiltered apple cider, preferably with no sugar added

1 teaspoon Herbes de Provence

1 tablespoon honey, maybe more depending on the sweetness of your apples

2 teaspoons fresh-cracked black peppercorns

2 large organic Fuji apples, medium diced

1 large organic Granny Smith apple, medium diced

1 tablespoon apple pectin

1 teaspoon sea salt

In a heavy-bottomed pot on medium heat, melt 1 tablespoon butter and caramelize the onions, stirring frequently. Once caramelized, add cider, herbs, honey, and pepper and let simmer.

In a sauté pan on high heat, melt the rest of the butter and sauté the apples until browned; you still want them to have texture. Set aside.

In a small bowl, whisk the pectin with about ¼ cup of water. Set aside.

Puree the onion mixture in the pot with a stick blender, or use a food processor. Mix until smooth, then stir in the apples, pectin, and salt. Let simmer for 20–30 minutes.

OLD-FASHIONED TOMATO SOUP

(MAKES 4-6 8-OUNCE SERVINGS)

Tomato soup just always seems to pair best with a grilled cheese sandwich, and the Grilled Cheeserie cooks up a monstrously good tomato soup. It relies on the tomatoes and herbs to give it body and flavor.

1 onion, medium diced

2 tablespoons butter

3 pounds ripe tomatoes or 1 (28-ounce) can tomatoes (preferably San Marzano)

1 tablespoon Benton's Bacon fat (or other smoky bacon of your choice)

1 teaspoon salt

1 tablespoon freshly ground black pepper

½ cup heavy cream

1 tablespoon sugar

Sweat onions in butter until translucent, then add tomatoes. Simmer about 1 hour.

Add bacon fat, salt, and pepper, then blend. Add cream and sugar and simmer on low heat for up to 2 hours.

HEMINGWAY'S BAR AND HIDEAWAY

438 Houston Street, Suite 160, Nashville
(615) 915-1715
hemingwaysbarandhideaway.com

Hemingway's delights me—and pretty much everyone else in Nashville, since it walked away with nearly every award the Nashville Scene could give a new restaurant in 2017. Set in the rapidly reviving Wedgewood Houston neighborhood, close to the new Corsair Distillery location and not far from the Fairgrounds and the speedway, Hemingway's is part of what makes this neighborhood a must-visit. It combines the warmth of a neighborhood restaurant with a little hint of speakeasy, and the casual grace that Nashville's best high-end restaurants seem to be adept at pulling off. Yes, it takes its inspiration from the work and life of Ernest Hemingway, and that's an excellent thing. It's open, comfortable, airy, and it's the kind of place you want to linger over dinner, drinks, and dessert.

The menu is on-trend and thoughtful, Southern with a whisper of French and Italian tradition—try risotto or beef tartare to start with, follow up with duck breast, short ribs (recipe follows) or chicken and dumplings. Specialty cocktails are the rule. Yes, there's good beer and wine, but really—check the cocktail menu here.

SHORT RIB STEW WITH FINGERLING POTATOES, CARROTS & PEARL ONIONS

This is one of the more complex recipes in the book, but trust me, it's worth the effort.

For the short ribs:

5 pounds bone-in short ribs, or 3 pounds boneless short ribs

For the fingerling potatoes:

1 pound fingerling potatoes

Canola oil

Salt to taste

For the pearl onions:

1 pound peeled pearl onions

Canola oil

Salt to taste

For the carrots:

1 pound carrots, peeled and diced

2 cups orange juice

¼ cup coriander seeds

2 ounces (½ stick) butter

For the stout jus:

Reserved cooking liquid from short ribs or 2 cups chicken stock

2 bottles Guinness or other traditional stout (avoid flavored stouts)

1 bunch thyme

⅛ cup black pepper

2 small carrots

1 medium onion

3 stalks celery

1 head garlic, cut in half

For the dish:

Canola oil

2–3 tablespoons butter

Salt & black pepper, to taste

To prepare the short ribs: In a roasting pan, cover the short ribs with water or chicken stock and cook at 300°F in your oven until short ribs are very soft but not falling apart, 3–4 hours. Alternately, you can vacuum pack the short ribs and cook sous vide at 185°F for 24 hours.

Remove the short ribs from your cooking vessel. Reserve short ribs and cooking liquid separately. When short ribs are completely cooled, remove the bones if necessary, and cut into large cubes, approximately 1 x 1-inch.

To prepare the fingerling potatoes: Toss the potatoes in oil and salt, roast in a 400°F oven until tender. Cool completely, then cut in half lengthwise.

To prepare the pearl onions: Toss the onions in oil and salt, roast in a 400°F oven until tender and lightly browned. Cool completely.

To prepare the carrots: In a small pot, cover the carrots with orange juice. Add coriander seeds and butter. Cook over low heat until the carrots are soft, but not overcooked. Strain and discard the liquid, reserving the carrots. Remove any excess coriander seeds. Cool carrots completely.

To prepare the stout jus: Combine all ingredients in a small stock pot. If you cooked the short ribs sous vide, you will need to add the optional chicken stock to the pot. If not, use the reserved liquid from your cook pot. Cook over low heat until reduced by about half. Strain out vegetables, reserving liquid.

To prepare the dish: In a large sauté pan over medium-high heat, brown the short rib pieces, working in batches if necessary. Add in the fingerlings, pearl onions, and carrots.

Add stout jus and return all the short rib pieces to the pan. Reduce cooking liquid until you reach your desired thickness, then add the butter to the pan. Swirl to emulsify the butter into the sauce.

Season to taste with salt and pepper and serve immediately.

HUGH BaBY'S

4816 Charlotte Avenue, Nashville
(615) 610-3340
3001 West End Avenue, Nashville
(615) 610-3382
hughbabys.com

Y'all, just when you think Pat Martin can't do it again, he does. I am unabashedly a fan of what he's done for Nashville's barbecue scene, and now he's at it again, teaming with Fresh Hospitality to bring us another take on good, old-fashioned sandwiches and Southern-style diner food. The menu is the kind of stuff your grandparents would have felt great ordering in the 1940s and '50s—heck, your great-grandparents might have recognized this food in the '20s and '30s. And it's delicious.

It's a Martin joint, you can always get perfect, slow-roasted hog barbecue. I mean, what else? Funny you should ask that, because if you want a terrific old-style burger—the Corinth, Mississippi–style slug burger (which blends meat with flour and grits, served with mustard, pickles, and onions, in that circa 1931 way) for example? Well, they're serving it up. And did we mention the shakes? So good! And hot dogs, fries, all-beef burgers—all of the food you crave, from an era before the obligatory fast food burger changed it.

When I asked Pat and his gorgeous wife Martha for a recipe you could master at home, the smoked chicken thigh sandwich was his immediate choice. I can't argue—this is the perfect summer dinner. It's made with Alabama-style white sauce, Pat's take on the Huntsville-Decatur, Alabama barbecue tradition that makes chicken just perfect. You're on your own for making the perfect fries, my friends. When you're in town, put Hugh Baby's on your must-lunch list!

SMOKED CHICKEN THIGH SANDWICH

(MAKES 4 SANDWICHES)

For the smoked chicken thighs:

4 boneless skinless chicken thighs, trimmed of any excessive fat

2 tablespoons of your favorite dry rub (Martin's Hoss Rub suggested)

For the white sauce:

1 cup mayo

⅓ cup apple cider vinegar

¼ cup apple juice

1 teaspoon white sugar

¾ teaspoon minced horseradish

¾ teaspoon black pepper

¾ teaspoon kosher salt

¾ teaspoon lemon juice

¾ teaspoon minced garlic

¼ teaspoon cayenne

To build the sandwich:

4 Buns

Sweet Hot pickles (Wickles Pickles suggested)

To prepare the smoked chicken thighs: Rub trimmed chicken thighs with the dry rub. Smoke the thighs on a tray at 250°F for approximately 1 hour or until the internal temperature reach 165°F.

To make the white sauce: Combine all ingredients and whisk together. You can also use an immersion blender for this.

To serve: Place chicken thighs on buns and top with White Sauce and Sweet Hot pickles.

Jasmine

8105 Moores Lane, Suite 1500, Brentwood
(615) 661-0169
jasminenashville.com

If I have a default restaurant at all, it's Jasmine. Set in a shopping plaza in Cool Springs—the rapidly growing space that bridges and merges Franklin and Brentwood in Williamson County—that also houses Publix and Home Depot, it may seem unprepossessing from the outside, but the interior is a welcome respite from suburban sprawl. The decor is simple and Asian with a contemporary American twist, the atmosphere is soothing, and the food is rich and flavorful.

My mother, sister, and I make Jasmine a regular family gathering spot, where we can get away from the guys and just talk. (I suspect the only place my mother ever really wants to eat at is Jasmine, regardless of the time or occasion.)

The menu's specialties are familiar to fans of Thai cuisine, but the flavors here seem more powerfully authentic than many similar places. I think they know by now when I call that my husband wants the garlic beef dish, and I need either the Hung Ray Curry or the ginger pork with mushrooms—all of it with level four heat, by personal request (yeah, we like it spicy). When the day's been especially stressful, Jasmine takeout is almost a necessity.

In recent years, sushi has taken over a sizable amount of the menu, some of the best in Williamson County, but I'm still here jumping over from my office at least one night a week to grab Pad Kee Mao or green curry takeout. There are many bigger and more plush Asian-themed restaurants in the city, but this one is special, as anyone who visits will tell you.

CUCUMBER SALAD

(SERVES 2)

Rice powder (instructions below)

Carrot Vinaigrette (recipe follows)

2 tablespoons crushed peanuts

1 whole large English cucumber

Kosher salt, to taste

Sugar, to taste

3 teaspoons fresh lime juice

Cilantro, for garnish

To prepare the rice powder: On low heat, sauté about ½ cup of uncooked rice for 10–12 minutes, until lightly browned. Remove from heat, and grind the rice to a fine powder.

To prepare the cucumber: Use a peeler to make ribbons.

To assemble the salad: In a bowl, mix the Carrot Vinaigrette, crushed peanuts, and rice powder. Use vinaigrette lightly so it doesn't pool in bottom of bowl. Add the cucumber ribbons and toss thoroughly. Season the salad with salt and sugar to taste and the fresh lime juice. Garnish the plate with chopped cilantro. Serve at once.

CARROT VINAIGRETTE

1 whole carrot

½ cup rice wine vinegar

1 teaspoon salt

1 teaspoon sugar

Thoroughly rinse the carrot, then shred the carrot completely.

Whisk together the rice wine vinegar, salt, and sugar. Add the shredded carrot and refrigerate overnight.

WILLIAMSON COUNTY

Just south of Nashville along I-65 lie the towns of Brentwood and Franklin, along with a cluster of smaller communities that make up Williamson County. While independent of the city of Nashville, many of Nashville's largest businesses, including Nissan North America and several major health-care companies, make their homes here, especially in suburban Cool Springs.

The county has a prodigious history and historic sites, including Carnton Plantation (made famous in Robert Hicks's NYT bestseller *The Widow of the South*), the Carter House and the Battle of Franklin site, the Harvey McLemore House, the Lotz House, and a downtown neighborhood of gorgeous historic homes. Quarterly street festivals in downtown Franklin draw enormous crowds. Outside Franklin and Brentwood, the local farm movement has become a tour de force supplier across the board from farmers' markets to Whole Foods.

Traditionally Williamson County, for all its financial wealth, was notable for its bland chain restaurants. That's changing dramatically: Area chefs such Nick Pellegrino (Mangia Nashville), Jason McConnell and Carl Schultheis (Red Pony, 55 South, Cork & Cow), Pat Martin (Martin's BBQ), and others have brought a paradigm shift, building the appetite for good local, chef-driven restaurants. Meanwhile, Nashville entrepreneurs have taken the plunge, opening much-loved locations such as Burger Up, , Local Taco, Cool Springs Brewery, and more in Williamson County.

Small spots like Puckett's Grocery have begun to expand Williamson restaurant empires into Nashville to return the favor by opening locations downtown. One of the early, old-school Nashville independent steak houses, Sperry's, opened doors in Cool Springs a few years ago.

Ethnic food has taken hold, too, from longtime resident Thai mainstay Jasmine to outstanding places like Mysore Palace, Bawarchi Biryani Pointe, Paradise Biryani, Wild Ginger, House of India, and a host of small sushi joints. In Brentwood, Corner Asian has a real Schezhan menu presented by Taiwan-trained chefs, something Williamson has never seen before.

In spite of its reputation for chains and suburban sprawl, a truly interesting and worthwhile culinary culture is taking hold. Add to that growing potential as wine country with Arrington Vineyards, and the beginnings of its own microbrew and distilling community, and there is every reason to be bullish about where Williamson goes from here.

Buttermilk

Sausage & Cheddar

Blueberry Marshmallow Cheesecake

Gluten Free

KITCHEN NOTES

250 5th Avenue South, Nashville
(in the Omni Hotel)
(615) 761-3700
kitchennotesnashville.com

Set inside the Omni Hotel downtown, Kitchen Notes masters breakfast and brunch like few places in the city (yes, you can get dinner and lunch too). The all-day biscuit bar is part of its charm. It's a Southern-inspired restaurant, according to the Omni Nashville Culinary Team, but those familiar with any style of classic American comfort food will find themselves at home here. The style is higher end than its splendid country cousins that abound as you move toward more rural Tennessee, but the taste is delicious and familiar.

I love the farm-to-table vibe that continues to grow, and Kitchen Notes keeps that going too. We're lucky in Nashville that local farms are readily available to provide for our chefs. Local partnerships with regional farms and artisan food producers, including The Nashville Jam Company, Tennessee Honey, and Black Hawk Farms, help define the restaurant's identity.

Here are a few recipes with a real Nashville energy—including some absolutely stellar biscuits to share with the people you really love.

CRANBERRY ORANGE BISCUITS

(SERVES 8-10)

2 ½ cups flour (White Lilly preferred)

⅓ cup sugar

2 teaspoons baking powder

½ teaspoon baking soda

Pinch salt

1 teaspoon orange zest

¾ cup dried cranberries

4 ounces unsalted butter (frozen)

1 cup milk or buttermilk, plus more for brushing

1 tablespoon sour cream

1 egg

1 teaspoon vanilla

Preheat oven 425°F regular or convection at 375°F.

In a large mixing bowl, combine flour, baking powder, baking soda and salt. Add dried cranberries and zest—make sure dispersed evenly. Grate butter just removed from freezer on a large hole of your box grater, into the dry ingredients. Lightly mix (the faster the better).

Briefly beat the egg; add to the buttermilk (or milk), along with the sour cream and vanilla. Stir until mixed.

Make a well in the center of the dry mix and pour all the chilled liquid in at once. Stir just until the dough comes together (dough should be sticky).

Turn dough onto floured surface, dust the top with flour, and gently roll- or pat out. Fold dough over on itself two times gently, rolling it out in between each fold. Lightly press into ¾-inch- to 1-inch-thick dough. Cut biscuits with a 2-inch cutter, being sure to push straight down through the dough. Do not twist. Start from the outside work inward when cutting.

Place biscuits on baking sheet about ¾ to 1 inch apart. Brush with a little buttermilk or heavy cream.

(The closer the biscuits are to each other, the taller they get—it will kind of look like a honeycomb.)

Bake until biscuits are tall and light gold on top, 10–15 minutes. Remove from oven serve immediately with fresh whipped cream, butter, or cranberry jam.

BUTTERMILK BISCUITS

(SERVES 8-10)

1¾ cups White Lilly flour

½ teaspoon salt

2 teaspoons baking powder

1 teaspoon sugar (optional, it adds just a hint of sweetness and some moisture)

½ teaspoon baking soda

5 tablespoons unsalted butter (frozen)

¾ cup buttermilk (or more as needed)

Preheat oven 425°F regular or convection at 375°F.

In a large mixing bowl combine all dry ingredients. Grate the butter just removed from freezer on the large hole of a box grater, into the dry ingredients. Lightly mix, the faster the better.

Make a well in the center and pour in the chilled buttermilk all at once. Stir just until the dough comes together—dough should be sticky. If you

need to add more buttermilk, do it quickly at this stage.

Turn dough onto a floured surface, dust top with flour, and gently roll out or pat out, fold dough over on itself two times gently rolling it out in between each fold. Lightly press into ¾-inch to 1-inch thick dough. Cut biscuits with a 2-inch cutter, being sure to push straight down through the dough. Do not twist. Start from the outside and work inward when cutting.

Place biscuits on baking sheet about ¾ to 1 inch apart. Brush with a little buttermilk or heavy cream. (The closer the biscuits are to each other, the taller they get. It will kind of look like a honeycomb.)

Bake until biscuits are tall and light gold on top, 10–15 minutes. Remove from oven serve immediately with fresh butter, jam and honey.

PANCAKES

(SERVES ABOUT 6)

2 eggs

¾ quart, plus 1 ounce buttermilk

3¼ ounce canola oil

2 cups flour

2 tablespoons granulated sugar

4 teaspoons baking powder

1 teaspoon baking soda

Combine eggs, buttermilk, and oil and mix well.

In a separate bowl, combine flour, sugar, baking powder, and baking soda evenly.

Blend dry ingredients into the egg mixture. *Do not overbeat or over mix.*

Refrigerate, covered with plastic wrap, for 15 minutes.

Use a 4-ounce scoop or ladle to portion the batter, and cook on a pre-heated, lightly oiled griddle or cast iron surface (griddle 350°F or about medium low heat on stove top with cast iron pan) until the tops of pancakes are covered with bubbles. Turn once. Cook until done.

MEATLOAF WITH MUSHROOM GRAVY

(SERVES 6-8)

For the mushroom gravy:

1 ounce shallots, minced

¾ tablespoon minced garlic

1¼ pounds Crimini mushrooms

1¼ pounds oyster mushrooms

¾ tablespoon chopped fresh thyme

2 ounces red wine

3 cups demi-glace (you can purchase at your
   favorite grocery, pre-made)

1 tablespoon red wine vinegar

1 teaspoon salt

½ teaspoon ground black pepper

For the Meatloaf:

½ onion, diced small

½ pound button mushrooms, sliced

1 tablespoon vegetable oil

1 ounce minced garlic

2 teaspoons Kosher salt

1 teaspoon black pepper

½ teaspoon fresh sage, finely chopped and rubbed

1 teaspoon fresh parsley, finely chopped

¼ loaf sliced white bread, crust removed torn into
   1-inch pieces

½ cup milk

½ cup beef stock

2 eggs

2½ pounds ground chuck, 80/20 prime grade beef

¾ pound fontina cheese, grated (optional)

To prepare the gravy: Sauté shallots until translucent. Add garlic and sauté until aromatic.

Add all mushrooms and thyme and sauté until tender and most of the moisture is removed.

Add red wine and reduce until *au sec* (almost dry). Add demi-glaze, red wine vinegar, salt, and pepper. Simmer gently until nice sauce consistency is achieved, this should not take long.

To prepare the meatloaf: Sweat onions and mushrooms in vegetable oil until soft; add garlic and continue to slowly cook for another 5 minutes. Add salt, pepper, sage, and parsley. Cool down in refrigerator.

Mix together bread, milk, beef stock, and eggs. Add cooled onion mix and ground beef, mix gently—and do not overmix—until all is incorporated. Cook a piece to check the seasoning and adjust if needed.

Place meatloaf mix in loaf pan lined with parchment paper, tap loaf pan down on table until compact. Cover top with cheese (if desired). Bake meatloaf covered at 300°F until it reaches 165°F in the center. Remove and let rest covered for a minimum of 10 minutes. Remove the meat loaf from the mold. Slice desired portions.

Serve with mushroom gravy, mashed potatoes and long cooked green beans or any of your favorite side dishes.

SPOTLIGHT ON MURFREESBORO

To the southeast of Nashville lies Rutherford County. Murfreesboro, home to Middle Tennessee State University and one of the fastest growing communities in Tennessee, with a population of more than 100,000 souls, became home to my husband and me in 2017. Just as rich in history as its neighbors, Rutherford County has been perhaps a little slow to move itself out of the realm of chain restaurants. That's changing, however. The large population and the area's growing role as a haven for Nashville business types who don't want to live in the city mean that more chefs and entrepreneurs are looking to Rutherford as a viable site for new and original locations.

Among the favorites are The Green Dragon Pub and Brewery—a marvelous public house with an incredible beer list and light meals that plays on themes from Tolkien's The Hobbit; the exquisite food stylings of high-end 5 Senses; Cajun cantina Blue Cactus; a lovely extension of Ohio-based micro-chain The Goat; and Wall Street, with a great bar and live entertainment. Nashville favorites like Party Fowl, Puckett's, Pfunky Griddle, and the local Brewhouse chain have now opened locations in the 'Boro. Good ethnic food, including The Clay Pit, Sabaidee, Fin Fusion, Tandoor, and the tiny Greek Café by the Kroger on 96—my favorites, among many others—is starting to abound.

The music and art scene thrives here, aided by the presence of a university that doesn't get the attention that UT does, but probably ought to, two centuries of history and architecture, a quaint antebellum courthouse square, and a diverse community, make this a city that is likely to grow in size and foodie options quickly. The growing farmers' markets bring out a crowd for local produce each week, too.

Mayday Brewery, and the forthcoming expansions by Mantra Artisan Ales and Sazerac also make the potable beverage culture something to watch closely. Mayday always seems to have live music— when I was there a bit ago, a National Endowment for the Humanities–recognized buck dancer gave an improvised performance with the local bluegrass band playing—and there's always a food truck outside.

Le Sel

1922 Adelicia Street, Nashville
(615) 490-8550
leselnashville.com

Pretty much everything the Goldberg brothers touch goes incredibly right, and Le Sel, their recent take on French brasserie dining, is a perfect example. The Midtown restaurant picks up on the trend toward delight in décor, including a scuba-ready bulldog statue that provoked giggles from me on my first visit. The menu, however, is a Francophile dream. Come here for bouillabaisse, stay for the côte du boeuf au poivre.

This recipe for moules frites by Chef Brian Lea is quintessentially French, and absolutely superb. If you want to impress guests with something elegant without spending far too much time on preparation this recipe is for you. If you have an open kitchen plan, this is one you can make right in front of them.

MOULES FRITES

(SERVES 2-4)

1 pound mussels

2 garlic cloves, sliced thin

1 shallot bulb, sliced

1 tablespoon canola oil

4 ounces dry white wine

1 sprig of fresh thyme

1 ounce butter

Pinch of salt

Lemon juice to taste (fresh)

2 tablespoons chopped herbs, like parsley, chive, tarragon, and chervil

Crusty baguette

Clean the mussels: Wash them under cold running water, giving them a light scrub. Check for the "beard"—the fibers that protrude from the mussels that allow them to cling to things. Grip it between your index finger and thumb, and pull down toward the hinge.

Tip: Discard any mussels with cracked shells or that don't begin to close with a tap on a hard surface.

In a medium sauté pan, sweat the garlic and shallots with the canola oil for two minutes on low heat, until they are translucent, but not browned. Carefully add the white wine to the pan, being sure not to cause a flame up. Cook off the alcohol from the wine, and add the mussels and thyme. Simmer at medium heat until half of the mussels are open, at which point you will add the butter. While still simmering, stir the butter into the mussels and cooking liquid. Season with salt, lemon juice and herbs. Once the mussels are all open, pour into a large bowl and serve with the baguette.

LOCKELAND TABLE,
A COMMUNITY KITCHEN AND BAR

1520 Woodland Street, East Nashville
(615) 228-4864
lockelandtable.com

Lockeland Table is an established mainstay guided by powerhouse chef Hal Holden-Bache. I first met him in barbecue god Patrick Martin's kitchen, along with Tyler Brown of Capitol Grille and Tandy Wilson of City House, cooking up a storm for a collection of friends several years ago. Prior to opening his own place, Hal spent time at the late and lamented Nick and Rudy's Steakhouse, then moved on to work at Capitol Grill with Tyler, and then to Eastland Cafe in East Nashville. In 2012 he finally took the plunge and opened up his own place.

Needless to say, Lockeland didn't disappoint—as its nomination as one of the best new restaurants of 2013 from the James Beard Foundation underlines. Not that we had any doubts.

The menu is a mix of the rustic and the refined; consider starters like skillet corn bread and Cox Farm roasted bone marrow (I love bone marrow, and this is superb) to a local cheese plate that lets you pick your own options.

For your main course, choose from a wealth of wood-fired pizzas, or heartier options like a New York strip steak or Carolina mountain trout with maple bourbon glaze. Side dishes range from pommes frites (of course) to grits to braised greens.

Keep your eyes on Hal—anyone who doubts this chef is going places hasn't eaten at his restaurant. And if you can't make it in, here are some real Southern sides to whet your appetite.

SOUTHERN CORN BREAD
(SERVES 6-10, DEPENDING ON THE SIZE OF SERVINGS)

4 cups cornmeal

4 cups all-purpose flour

1 teaspoon salt

¼ cup baking powder

4 eggs

2 cups margarine, melted

8 cups buttermilk

½ cup corn oil

Preheat oven to 375°F.

Mix all the ingredients thoroughly, except the corn oil.

Use the corn oil to grease your baking vessel (cast iron recommended but not required). Bake for 20 minutes or until golden brown.

COLLARD GREENS

(SERVES 6–8)

3 slices smoked bacon

1 yellow onion, diced

4 cloves garlic, chopped

1 shallot

1 cup chicken stock

1 Yazoo dos Perros*

10 dashes Tabasco

¼ cup apple cider vinegar

1 tablespoon granulated sugar

6 bunches collard greens, cleaned and chopped

Bring all the ingredients except the collard greens to a simmer in a thick-bottomed pot at low heat.

Add the collards. Cover and simmer for 2–12 hours. Adjust seasonings to taste.

*Note: Yazoo is a local brewing company whose products are increasingly available at specialty beer locations nationally. If you must substitute, use New Belgium Fat Tire or Dos Equis Amber.

THE LOVELESS CAFÉ

8400 Tennessee Highway 100, adjacent to Bellvue and Fairview
(615) 646-9700
lovelesscafe.com

I got my first tastes of the Loveless Cafe over a decade ago, when I was fresh out of grad school and doing regional theater, including performing at local standby Chaffin's Barn Dinner Theatre. The Loveless was just down the road, and often just what the tired actors wanted post-rehearsal. Ah, fried chicken.

By that time the Loveless already had decades of its own history behind it and a series of successful owners, each of which had taken it one step further as a restaurant of note. The most recent ownership has expanded it even further and renovated, but kept the same classic Southern-style feel to the menu that's had people coming back for sixty years or more.

The Loveless has grown to define what people really think Nashville cooking is all about over the years, and in that time they've set themselves up as solid purveyors of good, old–fashioned, home-cooking-style food. Brimming breakfast platters, complete with the restaurant's signature biscuits, make it a favorite breakfast locale.

Supper plates are heaped with standbys: barbecue pork, country-fried steak, traditional home-made meat loaf, fried chicken livers. Pair them with the beans of the day, homemade creamed corn, fried okra, stone-ground grits, or fried green tomatoes—you get the picture. This is serious comfort food.

In 2013 the Loveless got itself a new distinction, as the James Beard Foundation invited them to serve Valentine's Day dinner in the Beard House in New York, re-anointing the cafe as master-ful Tennessee traditional cookery.

As you know by now, side dishes are vital necessities in Southern cooking. This carrot pud-ding is a perfect side if you need to make sure your family members are getting their veggies, even as they devour something rich, creamy, and just faintly sweet.

Homemade desserts have made their place felt in the Loveless's menu, and any visit there had best be made with the intention of following your meal with a piece of pie or a slice of cake. If you don't go that route, you'll regret it for a long time.

The Goo Goo Cluster, for those not familiar, is a native chocolate bar, rich in peanuts, caramel, chocolate, and marshmallow. If you haven't had them yet, order a box at googoo.com.

CARROT PUDDING

(SERVES 10)

The Loveless really does side dishes right, and this one is a winner when its sweet lusciousness is paired with serious, savory entrees.

1½ teaspoons salt

4 pounds carrots, peeled and cut in thick slices

¼ pound unsalted butter, melted

½ orange, washed and zested

4 eggs, whipped by hand

1¼ cups sugar

⅓ cup all-purpose flour

1 tablespoon ground cinnamon

1 tablespoon baking powder

Preheat oven to 350°F.

Fill a large pot with water, add salt and boil the carrots until tender. Drain in a colander.

Mash the carrots thoroughly while hot by hand with a potato masher. Stir in the butter. Add the orange zest and squeeze in the orange juice (through a strainer). Stir well.

Add the eggs. Stir.

Fold in the sugar, flour, cinnamon, and baking powder (having previously mixed them together well). Stir until all ingredients are well blended.

Pour into a greased casserole dish. Bake until internal temperature reaches 175°F, approximately 40 minutes. Serve hot. Enjoy!

GOO GOO CLUSTER PIE

(MAKES 1 [9-INCH] PIE, SERVING 8)

3 egg whites

⅔ cup plus 2 tablespoons sugar, divided

¾ cup corn syrup

⅓ cup water

8 ounces semisweet chocolate

½ cup half-and-half

1 teaspoon vanilla extract

2 Goo Goo Clusters, chopped into small pieces

1 (9-inch) graham cracker pie shell

¼ cup chopped roasted unsalted peanuts

1 cup caramel sauce or dulce de leche

Place the egg whites in a large mixing bowl with 2 tablespoons of sugar and mix on low speed. Do not allow it to become frothy; simply mix it enough to dissolve the sugar.

Place the corn syrup and water in a small, heavy-bottomed pot with the remaining 2/3 cup of sugar. Set the pan over medium heat and stir to dissolve the sugar. Using a wet pastry brush, wash the sides of the pot so that no sugar crystals remain, and once the sugar is dissolved, do not stir it. Place a candy thermometer in the pot and cook until the mixture reaches 240°F. While the sugar cooks, you can use the time to make the chocolate ganache glaze.

To make the ganache, place the chocolate and half-and-half into a heatproof metal or glass bowl and set over water that is barely simmering. As it heats, whisk gently to melt the chocolate and make a smooth, glossy glaze.

Next, with a stand mixer on medium speed, whip the egg whites until they are frothy with soft peaks just beginning to form. While the mixer is whipping, carefully pour the hot sugar mixture into the bowl. Take great care to avoid hitting the beaters, or the hot sugar will splatter and can burn. Once all the sugar is added, allow the egg whites to whip fully, until big and fluffy and they resemble marshmallow cream, about 5–8 minutes.

Add the vanilla and continue to whip the marshmallow cream for another minute or two. Remove from mixer and fold in the chopped Goo Goo Cluster pieces.

To assemble the pie, pour 2–3 tablespoons of the chocolate ganache glaze into the bottom of the pie shell and tilt the pan to spread it evenly over the crust. Sprinkle half of the peanuts evenly over the glaze. Once the chocolate glaze is set, transfer the marshmallow Goo Goo filling into the prepared pie shell. Using an icing spreader, decorate the top of the pie with the remaining chocolate ganache glaze.

Top it off with the remaining peanuts and chill for at least 1 hour.

To serve, place slices on plates and drizzle each with 2 tablespoons of caramel sauce or dulce de leche.

NASHVILLE INFLUENCERS

Influencers come and go in any town, but if I have to pick two that have helped Nashville to grow and thrive, Melissa Corbin of Corbin in the Dell and Vivek Surti of VEA Supper Club come to mind.

Melissa founded Corbin in the Dell is 2012, "I've always had the itch to tell a good story and it was time to scratch it," said Corbin. "It was a now or never sort of notion, as I faced the next chapter in my life. Really, it's been one of the hardest things I've ever done, but also the most rewarding by far."

Those who follow her on social media get a dose not just of the Middle Tennessee farm-to fork culture she began to promote back then, but elements of the way farmers, food, and agriculture touch every aspect of American life across the country. If you want to understand what farm-to-fork really means, down in its bones, rather than as a rhetorical game, follow Melissa.

When I asked her what changes she'd seen over the past few years, this was her response—and it sums up so much why it's vital that foodies support agriculture:

"My father was one of the first farmers in Montgomery County to raise soybeans. He raised more than a few eyebrows in his day . . . much like hemp farmers are revolutionzing the industry today. Meanwhile, as the modern agrian community shrinks, this new crop of farmers is learning to do with far fewer acres out of necessity. They're not land heirs. They're doing with what they have, which makes it hard to survive. I suppose that part of agriculture hasn't changed much for the small, independent farm. As our community champions the current status of our culinary landscape, willing to plop down a whole day's wages for a proper meal, an egg producer can barely stay afloat as that same community scratches its head over a $6 per dozen price tag. Don't get me wrong, the restauranteurs and chefs are well-deserving of such status, but so are the farmers. The best way for the everyday consumer to lift up the farming community is to support restaurants, markets, and other resources who give a damn about their food sources."

She has thoughts on what makes our food culture special as well: "The meat and three is a true Nashville original, as is hot chicken. That doesn't mean that's all we can do well. From biscuits and corn bread to whisky and brews, our food culture can't even begin to fit in a mere mason jar. Our cultures are just as diverse as other parts of the country, sit yourself down at the table and spark up a conversation." Find more at corbininthedell.com

If you remember the first edition of this book, supper clubs were just coming into their own. Most of my supper club folks, like Nick Pellegrino and Avon Lyons have moved on to larger culinary endeavors. Vivek Surti of VEA Supper Club, however, embodies both the supper club done right ethos we need and the same ebullient attitude toward mixing our local and regional traditions with a new international flair that seems to be burgeoning everywhere.

He says, "The idea of VEA Supper Club started after watching a one-hour special on the Cooking Channel about The Four Coursemen—a supper club held by friends in Athens, Georgia. The idea of going to a farm, picking out ingredients, building a menu, pairing that menu with wine, and showcasing it to guests with the farmer in attendance was super cool to me. I had just moved back from Washington, D.C. and so I figured, why not do this and make a little cash on the side? In May 2011, I hosted the first VEA Supper Club in my parents' house, and did about five events there before moving to Nashville Farmers Market. At NFM, I was lucky to partner with a good friend, Chef Laura Wilson, as we started hosted monthly dinners for twenty-five in 2012. In 2014, we started popping up in restaurants around town, and in 2015, started playing around with different experiences beyond our traditional five courses with wine pairings format."

The format has grown in options: "Our traditional format is a small, intimate gathering of twenty to thirty people with snacks, five plated courses and wine/cocktail/beer pairings. Our second format was to offer guests a more casual version of VEA Supper Club—less formal, one or two dishes, more people. We wanted to have the same quality of food but offer it to folks at a reasonable price ($20–$25).

"Third is a full restaurant takeover. This is where we go into a restaurant for a night, work with them on a menu, and sell it a la carte. Our first time, I was lucky to cook alongside James Beard Award–Winning Chef, Tandy Wilson at City House for Sunday Supper. At these dinners, the menu is more of a collaboration—we try to keep the philosophy of the host restaurant and incorporate my flavors/spices into the menu. Lastly, we do private dinner parties. So if someone wants the experience in their home, we'll come to you and work on a custom menu."

Vivek sums up what it is to celebrate immigrant tradition in the South and to blend cultures so brilliantly. This is the thing I think I'm most in love with about what he, Maneet Chauhan, and others are doing right now.

"My growth has really occurred in the development of me being able to tell my story through food. When I started, I cooked a lot of different cuisines and was figuring out a lot of things—how to feed a crowd, how to develop menus, how to position myself to execute a dinner successfully. I'm also a social science nerd, so I was constantly looking at the cultures behind the cuisine and what they represent. Looking back, I can see through the menus where my head was at.

"Seven years later, I'm a more confident cook with a precise definition of my style of cooking. I call it South Asian American Food. I don't call it Indian, because I believe that Indian food in this country makes people think of chicken tikka masala, naan bread, and rice. These dishes aren't even Indian and really hamper the ability of Indian cuisine to progress. Indian food, in my opinion, is the most regionally diverse food in the world. India is a country of more than twenty-nine states, each with different cultures, religions, cuisines and growing climates.

"The immigrant generation—mostly my parents' generation—came to America to earn a better life and provide a better foundation in life for their children. When they started Indian restaurants, they cared about making money and paying their bills by producing Indian food for Americans. Later, we started to see creative immigrant chefs do fusion cuisine. They came to America and saw Mexican food, Italian food, American food and said—why can't we incorporate some Indian flavors into these cuisines?

"The next story, I believe, is the one of first-generation Americans, like myself. My parents, grandparents, and family taught me the importance of knowing my Indian heritage, culture, and traditions. For an Indian American, I don't cook Indian food for Americans or Indian fusion food. I want to make food that is true to its heritage. We may present it differently or adjust the cooking technique, but the heart, soul, and flavor of a dish must come through."

VEA Supper Club is open to everyone: Sign up for the email list at VEASupperClub.com. Visit them @VEASupperClub on Instagram and Facebook.

MANGIA NASHVILLE

701 Craighead Street, Berry Hill
(615) 750-5233
facebook.com/MangiaNashville

At the original writing of this book, we were kind of catching on to the pop-up concept now, thanks to Nick Pellegrino's Mangia Nashville. Pellegrino is an amazing chef, but he relocated to Nashville for the music business, at which he's been rather successful. The problem was, there was nothing in the city remotely like the New York Italian food he was so used to eating. He began cooking for thrilled family and friends, and eventually hit upon the notion of a weekly pop-up to share, on a small scale, the kind of meals he grew up with.

Now, he's got his own premises in Berry Hill—near the Melrose district, but the wonders of his pop-up continue for weekend feasts. Sure, there's a more staid lunch hour and excellent weeknight dinners, but reservation-only weekend dinners—probably better to call them feasts—maintain the joy of the original. Lest you ask, regular lunch or dinner the food is always fantastic. What about the feasts? Well, over the course of three hours, you'll be served an epic, family-style meal like nothing you've had before, full of pasta and succulent lemon-rosemary chicken, or seasonal baked fishes, or skewers of perfect shrimp.

It's not just the seasonally changing menu—which is marvelous—but the ambiance when you come to a feast: You're often seated with complete strangers, who will be friends by the end of the night. Your wine is served in tiny glasses of a kind you haven't seen since *The Godfather*. Mid-meal, the whole crowd gets up and dances, led by Chef Nick beating on a kitchen pot with a wooden spoon, to everything from '50s mambo to '60s Jersey bands like Frankie Valli and the Four Seasons. By the time you leave, you can't believe how much you ate—and that's okay. Mangia is meant to be a night of wild joy, and it pulls it off, every time.

PENNE WITH PORCINI COGNAC CREAM SAUCE

(SERVES 4-6)

"This is one of the richest pasta dishes we make at Mangia Nashville," says Chef Nick. "The earthy flavor of the mushrooms combined with the cognac, the cream, and the cheeses are almost sinful. I have had customers ask for a straw so they could drink the leftover sauce. Who am I to tell them no?"

2 ounces dried porcini mushrooms

2 cups cognac or brandy, divided

1 cup warm water

6 tablespoons unsalted butter

3 cups heavy cream

1 cup grated Parmesan cheese

1 cup grated Pecorino Romano cheese

1 pound penne pasta, cooked al dente

Salt and freshly ground black pepper to taste

3 tablespoons fresh chopped chives, for garnish

Put the mushrooms, 1 cup of cognac, and warm water into a bowl and let soak until mushrooms are soft, about 20 minutes. Drain the mushrooms, reserving the liquid, and coarsely chop.

In a large skillet or saucepan, melt butter over medium heat. Add mushroom and sauté for 2 minutes. Add remaining cognac to the pan, raise the heat, and let reduce. Once most of the liquid is gone, add the water and cognac that the mushrooms were soaking in. (Be careful not to dump in any grit that might be at the bottom of the bowl from the mushrooms.)

Let this simmer until most of the liquid is reduced.

Add heavy cream to pan and gently simmer till reduced by half and it coats the back of a spoon. Stir in both cheeses.

Toss with penne, making sure that sauce covers all the pasta. ("I like to put a teaspoon of butter in at this point. It's already rich—why not drive right off the cliff?" says Chef Nick.)

Season with salt and pepper, transfer to a serving bowl, garnish with fresh chives, and enjoy!

ZEPPOLE

(MAKES ABOUT 35 ZEPPOLE)

"Some of my fondest childhood memories are of my family and I strolling through the San Gennaro Feast with a bag of freshly fried zeppole," Chef Nick reminisces. "I didn't even know who San Gennaro was or what he did, all I cared about was that I was getting zeppole! I knew that if I was to serve them, they could only be presented one way: in a white paper sack filled with confectionary sugar, just like they did at the feast. These have become our signature dessert, and at the end of every night you can see and hear everyone in the place shaking their little white bags. A night at Mangia Nashville is not over till the zeppole have been shaken."

1 quart vegetable oil for frying

1 cup all-purpose flour

2 teaspoons baking powder

Pinch of salt

1½ teaspoons white sugar

2 eggs, beaten

1 cup ricotta cheese

¼ teaspoon vanilla extract

½ cup confectioners' sugar for dusting

Heat oil in a heavy saucepot to 325°F. (Of course, you can use a deep fryer if you have one.)

In a medium saucepan over low heat, combine the flour, baking powder, salt, and sugar. Stir in the eggs, ricotta cheese, and vanilla. Mix till combined. The batter will be sticky. (This can be done several hours ahead of time and fried later. Store in the fridge lightly covered with plastic wrap to prevent a crust from forming.)

Using an ice-cream scoop, drop the zeppole into the oil a few at a time. They will turn over themselves when the first side is done. Fry till the second side is golden brown, about 3 minutes or so. Drain on a cooling rack set over a sheet pan. Transfer warm to paper sacks with confectioners' sugar. Shake and enjoy.

Marché

1000 Main Street, East Nashville
(615) 262-1111
marcheartisanfoods.com

Set right at the apex of the historic Five Points section of East Nashville, Marché is a favorite for just about everyone in the city. The European-style cafe offers up the best in fresh foods daily, from breakfast through dinner, and a fine brunch on Saturday and Sunday (typically packed!). They offer an artisan food market as well, including breads from regional bakers, fresh pastries and cookies to go, locally made Olive & Sinclair chocolates, and a host of similar items residents appreciate.

The atmosphere is open—there's plenty of glass, and the layout allows for a feeling of space. It's one of those restaurants where you're just as comfortable sitting alone and reading while you sip your coffee and relish your meal as you are with a crowd beside you.

I admit I'm usually ordering salads at Marché, because they are always seasonal, innovative, and delicious. But it's typically hard to resist the varying crepes du jour and the ever-changing seasonal entrees—in spring, for example, look for the lamb burger or an egg salad sandwich, while cooler months might bring an open-faced steak sandwich, Moroccan lamb stew, or a pan-seared hanger steak served with mushrooms and bacon grits.

Of the salad she's provided for the book, McCormack says: "This is on the menu at Marché every spring, and at Margot Cafe often as well. It's one of my favorites."

SALAD WITH FRESH STRAWBERRIES, BLUE CHEESE, TOASTED ALMONDS & WHITE BALSAMIC VINAIGRETTE

(MAKES 1 SALAD, WITH EXTRA DRESSING)

1½ teaspoons almonds

½ cup fresh salad greens (just picked are the best!)

5 fresh strawberries, quartered

1 tablespoon crumbled blue cheese (Your choice, but Marché uses a gorgonzola.)

White Balsamic Vinaigrette (recipe follows)

Begin by toasting the almonds lightly in the oven at 350°F for just a few minutes until they are golden brown. Prepare the salad greens by washing and drying thoroughly.

Toss the greens, almonds, strawberries, and blue cheese in an ample bowl. Drizzle the dressing lightly over the greens. (About an ounce per salad is the general rule of thumb—you don't want a soggy salad.) Gently toss together and serve immediately.

WHITE BALSAMIC VINAIGRETTE

(MAKES 12 OUNCES)

½ cup white balsamic vinegar*

2 cups vegetable oil

Pinch of salt

1 small shallot, minced

1 teaspoon Dijon mustard

1 teaspoon honey for a little sweetness

Pour the vinegar in a bowl and slowly whisk in the vegetable oil. (Margot prefers vegetable to the heavy olive oil, but you may use that instead if you prefer.) Whisk in salt, shallot, Dijon, and honey.

*Note: You can use any vinegar you like, but the sweetness and color of the white balsamic is the best for fruit preparations.

EAST NASHVILLE

In the early nineteenth century, as Nashville grew up along the Cumberland, wealthier families headed to the east side of the river, building estate homes and genteel farms away from the burgeoning city. In the middle of the century, a host of businesses cropped up, including furniture factories and their requisite sawmills; the area's commerce flourished. Middle-class neighborhoods expanded, and suburban areas were annexed.

The twentieth century brought a host of disasters: A massive fire in 1916 destroyed more than 500 homes and left thousands homeless, the Cumberland River floods of 1926–'27 wrecked property, and a huge tornado in 1933 damaged or destroyed more than 1,600 buildings. The 1940s through '60s saw efforts at "urban renewal," the noisy construction of the interstates, and the fight against school segregation that changed the demographics and popularity of this part of the city.

In the late '70s and '80s, the community began to revive, and especially after the 1998 Nashville tornado, a collection of businesspeople and an artisan community rediscovered the area's appeal. Now, East Nashville booms, with one of the most rapidly growing artisan restaurant and food cultures in town.

The outlying areas are home to plenty of farms, old and new. A weekly farmers' market has developed, and local groceries such as the Turnip Truck have emphasized the appeal of fresh, healthy foods to area residents. The trend toward home gardening and canning thrives in East Nashville right now, even as it slowly spreads across the rest of the city. The small but growing, Illinois-based Galena Garlic Company, purveyor of killer spice blends, just opened in the neighborhood, and is selling in a brick-and-mortar plus all the farmers' markets. I now have a full cabinet, and know where to find more.

The past ten to fifteen years have seen the area's restaurant culture flourish, starting with the dynamic Margot McCormack's Margot Cafe and places like Rosepepper Cantina. New restaurants seem to open daily, with restaurateurs like Jason McConnell, well established in other neighborhoods, opening places here. The arrival of Fat Bottom Brewery and Olive & Sinclair Artisan Chocolate, and custom businesses like the Bloomy Rind and Porter Road Butcher, all sourcing their wares to area restaurants, have built the area's reputation. Likewise, folks drive in from Franklin, Green Hills, and West End to hit art galleries, festivals, and boutiques, as well as dine at Silly Goose, Jeni's Splendid Ice Creams, Sweet 16th, Mad Donna's, Pharmacy Burger, and more.

Margot Café

1017 Woodland Street, East Nashville
(615) 227-4668
margotcafe.com

Chef Margot McCormack is something of a legend in Nashville. A Culinary Institute of America grad, she is also one of the true "Nashville Originals." Margot helped define local fine dining along with her eponymous restaurant, one of the first to locate in the East Nashville neighborhood in 2001, during its early revival. The building dates to the '30s and was a service station back in the day, set at the heart of Five Points (now just across from McCormack's newer venture, Marché).

Specializing in French country and rustic Italian cuisine, Margot is one of the few area restaurants that emphasize that classical European menu style; it's only recently that the city has really embraced truly French country cookery. Provence and Tuscany shine out from the exceptional daily changing menu that always maintains a solidly established number of appetizers, entrees, and desserts. A strong bar and wine list complements the menu, with a wide variety of price options and a notable representation of French and Italian options.

The vibe is warm, inviting, and decidedly European in decor and manner. The hidden brick porch is a lovely place to spend a spring evening or a crisp fall one. Simply put, no place else in Nashville is quite Margot.

On a regular menu, you might find an herb-infused olive oil with Parmigiano-Reggiano for dipping bread, house-made potato chips with aioli, a first course of mussels with roasted red pepper sauce and toasts, and entrees including pan-roasted steelhead, grilled lamb chops, and a vegetable pistou.

Of this dish, Margot says, "I love our chicken! This is a very simple preparation highlighting peas, which are one of my favorite things to look forward to each year."

CHICKEN WITH FRESH SPRING PEAS, POTATOES, LEMON & MINT

Per guest to be served:

3 fingerling or small red potatoes

About 1 tablespoon vegetable or olive oil

Salt and pepper

1 chicken breast

⅓ cup fresh peas

Pinch of minced shallot

1 tablespoon butter

1 sprig mint

¼ lemon wedge

Preheat oven to 400°F.

Drizzle potatoes with oil and sprinkle with salt. Roast until they are just soft. Slice the potatoes while still hot, but cool enough to work with. Set aside and keep warm.

In a pan over medium heat, sear the skin side of the chicken until golden brown, then season with a little salt and pepper. Transfer to a 400°F oven to finish cooking. (Use the still-hot oven the potatoes were in.)

While the chicken is cooking, sauté the peas in a warm pan with a pinch of shallot, butter, and fresh mint. Season with salt and pepper.

When the chicken is done to your liking—about 20 minutes cooking time—take out of the oven.

Place 5 or so slices of potatoes on a plate and spoon the peas on top. Place chicken over the vegetables and squeeze with a little lemon. (Margot says she uses their preserved lemon for extra goodness and often enjoys a little crumbled feta over the top as well.)

Martin's Bar-B-Que Joint

7238 Nolensville Road, Nolensville
(615) 776-1856
martinsbbqjoint.com

A few years ago, Tennessee native Pat Martin got tired of his landscaping business and decided he wanted to chuck it all and open a barbecue place—the real old-style kind, where whole hogs were roasted all day in the pit. Fortunately for Pat, his wife, Martha, decided this was a good idea, not a pipe dream. Martin found himself a location almost by accident in Nolensville, south of Nashville in Williamson County. When he outgrew that space just a few years later, he built a newer, bigger joint across the street, this one with a real hog pit, so guests can watch as the staff does the cooking—and more importantly, they can smell it.

Things have gone well, and these days Martin is a regular at Big Apple Barbecue, Charleston Food and Wine, and plenty of other national events. He's been featured on *Diners, Drive-Ins and Dives*. And the accolades keep coming.

In spite of that, Pat maintains his commitment to real barbecue, done the old-fashioned way, with the right kinds of sides. When you go, you have to order the pinto beans—just trust me—and make sure you also get an order of barbecue chicken with Alabama white sauce (Martin's is the best, even if it's made in Tennessee).

But the real deal here is hickory-smoked pork. Eat it. Eat lots. It's that good.

Martin provided the instructions for putting together one of his best dishes, the Redneck Taco, but assembly isn't the real thing—you'll need to cook your pork butt in your smoker with hickory. If you can't do that, then go out and buy it pre-smoked from someone who does.

REDNECK TACO

"It's assumed the reader has his/her own versions of pork, slaw, and red sauce," says Martin. I'll let you in on a secret: Your slaw must be light on mayo, heavy on flavor, and Sweet Dixie is a sweet heat–style sauce, so buy accordingly.

(MAKES 1 TACO)

½ cup prepared corn bread mix

1 tablespoon butter, melted

5 ounces pulled pork

4 ounces coleslaw

3 ounces Sweet Dixie sauce, or your favorite sauce

Drop prepared corn bread mix on griddle. With edge of cup, spread it evenly. Allow to cook for about 2 minutes 45 seconds. Carefully flip to other side.

Spread melted butter on top with a brush. Allow to cook for an additional 1 minute 45 seconds. Then plate.

Place pulled pork on top of warm hoecake, then place slaw on top of pulled pork. Pour Sweet Dixie or your favorite sweet-hot sauce on top and serve.

Mas Tacos Por Favor

732 B Mcferrin Avenue (brick-and-mortar location and food truck)
(615) 543-6271
facebook.com/mastacos

We all got used to seeing Teresa Mason's fabulous taco truck hanging out around Imogene + Willie in 12South and downtown, as well as East Nashville, long before there was a brick-and-mortar location we could access readily (that came in 2010). Like most cities in the South, Nashville was slow to touch upon the food truck scene, but Mason was one of our pioneers.

The atmosphere at the Mas Tacos shop is delightful. There's a certain amount of blended Mexican and retro '70s kitsch—with mismatched vintage tables, chairs, and stools; splashes of bright color in art and paint; and heavenly smells emanating from the window to the kitchen—that makes you feel you've still got the truck experience.

If you're there for lunch, chances are you're surrounded by a laughing crowd of people, but the noise level isn't bothersome. It's simply an indication that everyone here is *really* enjoying themselves, and you should, too.

Order your individual tacos from chalkboard menus, grab a Mexican Coke or a Jarritos soda, and you're good to go. Chicken, pork, fish—the tacos of your choice await, paired with fried plantains, black beans or avocados, or perhaps a little chile verde. Everything is delicious. The flavors are balanced and nuanced—it's everything you could want from a taco shop, and would be at home in L.A. as much as Nashville.

This chicken tortilla soup is incredibly popular. I've eaten it more times than I can count, and every single one has been great. Serve as a starter or use it as a main dish with a collection of complementary sides. Count it as spicy comfort food—and the plus side of the spice is that it makes for good summer eating, too.

CHICKEN TORTILLA SOUP

(SERVES 6–8)

1 (4-pound) chicken

1 onion, quartered

5 cloves garlic, smashed

2 habanero peppers

1 jalapeño pepper (with seeds), halved lengthwise

½ bunch cilantro

3 tablespoons (or more) fresh lime juice

Kosher salt and freshly ground black pepper

For garnish: fresh cilantro, halved cherry tomatoes, avocado wedges, queso fresco, warm soft tortillas, and grilled corn

Bring chicken, onion, garlic, peppers, and about 16 cups water to a boil in a large pot; skim foam from the surface. Reduce heat to medium and simmer, skimming the surface frequently, until chicken is cooked through, about 1 hour.

Transfer chicken from broth. Strain broth into another large pot. Return peppers to broth; discard remaining solids.

Shred chicken meat; discard skin and bones. Transfer chicken meat to a plate and set aside.

Meanwhile, set pot with strained broth over medium heat and add cilantro sprigs. Bring broth to a simmer and cook until reduced to 8 cups, about 1 hour. Discard sprigs.

Stir in lime juice. Season with salt, pepper, and more lime juice, if desired. Add chicken to broth; serve in bowls. Pass the garnishes so guests may top as they please.

MASON'S AND MASON BAR

2100 West End Avenue (Loews Vanderbilt Hotel, Midtown/West End)
(615) 321-1990
masons-nashville.com

Mason's and Mason Bar, the newly opened fine-dining establishment in the Loews Vanderbilt Hotel on West End Avenue, is a welcoming alternative to a lot of higher end chains that thrive around Vanderbilt.

The menu melds Southern food with modern fusion cuisines. It's about Southern style with a modern focus, done extraordinarily well. Add to that, a commitment to sourcing locally and seasonally as much as possible and you have a recipe for something good. Sourcing from local producers such as Provence breads and Kenny's Farmhouse Cheeses helps make a good menu even better.

Mason's Bar is also someplace you'll feel comfortable kicking back after a long day in the office. The cocktail menu is original, and tends toward re-envisioned classics.

This recipe might not be something you'd typically make at home, but be fearless—this is worth it. The Romesco will likely pair well with other dishes, especially when fresh tomatoes are in season. It's the brainchild of founding chef Brandon Frohne, who has moved on to a role at Holler and Dash, but whose mark is left indelibly, and whose chef-heirs are keeping up the traditions he started and building on them admirably.

BEEF TARTARE WITH PECAN ROMESCO

(SERVES 4)

2 anchovy fillets

1 teaspoon barrel-aged bourbon hot sauce

2 cloves garlic, chopped

½ cup minced shallots

1 tablespoon drained, chopped capers

2 tablespoons Dijon mustard

¼ cup olive oil

1 teaspoon Worcestershire sauce

1 pound beef tenderloin, minced

⅛ teaspoon kosher salt

1 tablespoon cracked black pepper

2 tablespoons Pecan Romesco (recipe follows)

In a chilled mixing bowl, mash the anchovies, hot sauce, and garlic with a fork to make a paste. Add the shallots and capers and mash them into the paste. Whisk in the mustard.

In a slow, steady stream, add the olive oil, whisking constantly until incorporated. Whisk in the Worcestershire sauce. Add the beef and mix well with a spoon. Season to taste with salt and pepper.

Spoon some tartare on top of the Romesco using a ring mold.

Optional: Garnish with shaved black truffle and crispy potato chips.

PECAN ROMESCO

(MAKES 2 CUPS)

1 head garlic

1 cup extra virgin olive oil, divided

12 toasted pecans

12 toasted hazelnuts

1 slice stale bread

2 ripe medium-size tomatoes or 1 large tomato

2 large roasted red peppers, well-drained

½ cup sherry vinegar

Kosher salt to taste

Roast garlic by first rubbing off excess dry skin from garlic head. Then place on a baking sheet and drizzle 1 tablespoon of olive oil on top. Roast in the oven for 20 minutes at 300°F or until garlic on inside is roasted and soft.

Place toasted pecans and hazelnuts into a food processor and process until finely ground.

Pour 2 tablespoons of olive oil into a small frying pan and quickly fry bread until both sides are browned. Remove from pan and allow to cool on a plate or paper towel.

Cut tomatoes into eighths and sauté in the same pan, adding oil if needed. Sauté for 4–5 minutes. Remove pan from heat.

Once bread is cooled, tear into pieces and process with the nuts. Add sautéed tomatoes and continue to process. Squeeze roasted garlic from the skins into the processor. Place roasted red peppers into the processor with the other ingredients and process until ingredients are a thick puree.

While processor is running, slowly drizzle in the remaining olive oil and the vinegar. Add salt to taste.

To plate the dish: Mound a circle of 2 tablespoons romesco on a plate, top with 3 ounces tartare mixture that has been molded in a cookie cutter. At the restaurant, Chef Brandon says he adds basil oil to garnish that's optional for an extra burst of herbaceous flavor. You can purchase basil olive oils at most specialty gourmet stores if you wish to add this step.

MCCABE PUB

4410 Murphy Rd, Nashville,
(615) 269-9406
mccabepub.com

McCabe Pub is practically a Nashville institution. Ain't no one in this town who hasn't had a beer here. This is, of course, because it has some of the best happy hours in town, and its menu of traditional all-American standards has consistently reigned in the realm of local pub food since 1982.

McCabe is set in West Nashville's Sylvan Park, not far from Pennington's Distillery on 44th Avenue North and is easily accessed via I-40 and 440. It's a wonderful neighborhood that locals know and tourists often miss. I like it for the cozy atmosphere and the fact that I never get a bad burger. The patio doesn't hurt—easily one of the best in the neighborhood, if not the whole city. It's a kick-back, get a local craft beer and a burger kind of place.

The recipe they've shared is a Southern staple, but it's one on which everyone in Tennessee and Kentucky possesses their own take on it. The great secret is that everyone in Kentucky and Tennessee has a bourbon pecan pie of some sort (yes, it's anathema to call Jack Daniels "bourbon," because this isn't Kentucky and we use a Lincoln County process, but by mash bill, it's comparable with many bourbons).

If you want to make this really right—buy your eggs from a local farmer. The taste change and the richness cannot be denied. (I get mine at the Murfreesboro or Franklin Farmers' Markets.) I also use butter from a local farm, just for the record.

JACK DANIEL'S CHOCOLATE PECAN PIE

(MAKES 1 [9-INCH] PIE THAT SERVES 6–8)

½ (15-ounce) package refrigerated piecrusts

4 large eggs

1 cup light corn syrup

6 tablespoons butter or margarine, melted

½ cup granulated sugar

¼ cup firmly packed light brown sugar

2 ounces Jack Daniel's whiskey*

1 tablespoon all-purpose flour

1 tablespoon vanilla extract

1 cup coarsely chopped pecans

1 cup semisweet chocolate morsels

Fit pie crust into a 9-inch pie plate according to package directions. Fold edges under and crimp.

Whisk together eggs, light corn syrup and next six ingredients in large bowl until mixture is smooth. Stir in chopped pecans and morsels. Pour into piecrust.

Bake on lowest oven rack at 350°F for 1 hour or until set.

*Option: Substitute 2 tablespoons butter or margarine, melted, if desired.

Merchants Restaurant

401 Broadway, West End
(615) 254-1892
merchantsrestaurant.com

In 2010 brothers Ben and Max Goldberg, having already made a name for themselves with the Patterson House, elegant event space Aerial, and a number of other properties through their company Strategic Hospitality LLC, decided to give Merchants a go. The restaurant, once a major fine-dining site in the city on the prominent part of Broadway, had been drifting toward obscurity for years at that point, well after its 1980s and '90s heyday. The brothers purchased the place, in its hundred-year-old building, and decided to revitalize the concept. That turned out to be inspired thinking.

Today's Merchants Restaurant is lighter, warmer, and more welcoming than the old version, and the food is designed to appeal to a vital, younger, more culinary-aware crowd. Perhaps the Goldbergs' most clever choice was essentially creating two restaurants in one: a bright, casual, bistro-esque dining first floor, and a low-lit, more "fine dining" establishment above.

The menus on the two floors vary as well. Downstairs, amid the black-and-white floor tiles, guests nosh on the favorite duck fat tater tots (I haven't had anything else like them that didn't come from a vendor on a French beach), bacon cheeseburgers, blackened tilapia, jambalaya, and the excellent chili recipe provided here. Upstairs, you're more likely to opt for beef tartare, a 14-ounce rib eye, scallops, or roasted pork tenderloin. The Strawberry Salad recipe comes from this side of the restaurant, and makes for a lovely starter before a fish or meat course, especially in spring, when the berries are fresh.

STRAWBERRY SALAD

(SERVES 4–6)

A couple of decades ago, Tennessee counted strawberries as one of their major crops. Sumner County, just north of Metro Davidson County, where Nashville proper sits, still grows vast quantities, and Portland, Tennessee, has an annual strawberry festival. It's likewise not surprising that

we like our strawberries used any way possible, like this strawberry vinaigrette, served over greens with goat cheese crumbles, which blends the berries' sweetness with the rich bitterness of the balsamic vinegar.

6 ounces mixed greens

2 ounces crumbled goat cheese

1 tablespoon minced red onion

2 tablespoons spicy pecans

¼ cup strawberries

Strawberry Vinaigrette (recipe follows)

Toss the salad ingredients together, and dress with vinaigrette.

Adding chicken or salmon (as shown) makes this tasty salad a heartier choice—Merchants recommends it.

STRAWBERRY VINAIGRETTE
(MAKES 24 OUNCES)

1 cup strawberry puree

½ cup balsamic vinegar

¼ cup red wine vinegar

6 tablespoons honey

1½ cups vegetable oil

½ cup olive oil

In a blender, combine strawberry puree, vinegars, and honey. Blend at a medium speed for 1 minute. Slowly add the oils to the mixture, and blend until thoroughly combined.

JOHNNY CASH'S "OLD IRON POT" FAMILY-STYLE CHILI
(SERVES 8-10)

Ah, chili—sometimes you just can't go wrong with the classics. You don't have to make this in cast iron, but it won't hurt a bit if you do. This recipe should make chili lovers happy.

For the chili spice blend:

¼ cup paprika

¾ cup Mexene Chili Powder

1 tablespoon cayenne

3 tablespoons cumin

2 tablespoons Chef Paul Prudhomme Blackened Redfish Magic

¼ cup sugar

¼ cup salt

For the chili:

2½ pounds ground beef

2 cups minced raw onions

½ cup minced poblano chile peppers

½ cup minced red bell pepper

½ cup tomato paste

3 cups pureed tomatoes

3 cups whole tomatoes

2 cups water

1 Tall Boy (24-ounce) Pabst Blue Ribbon Beer

3 cups cooked red kidney beans

Salt and pepper to taste

In a small bowl, combine the ingredients for the chili spice blend and mix thoroughly.

Brown the ground beef. Add onion and peppers, cooking until translucent. Add ½ cup of the chili spice blend and tomato paste. Cook for 5 minutes.

Add tomatoes, water, and PBR. Bring to a boil and return to a simmer. Let simmer for 1 hour.

Add kidney beans and simmer for 20 minutes. Salt and pepper to taste.

MIDTOWN CAFÉ

102 19th Avenue South, Midtown
(615) 320-7176
midtowncafe.com

Like Cabana and Sunset Grill, Midtown Cafe has evolved from the fine pairing of restaurateur Randy Rayburn and Chef Brian Uhl. Unlike their other ventures, Midtown is set in the heart of—you guessed it—Midtown, and you'll usually find the place packed for weekday lunches and dinners as a result, as it brings in the business clientele from West End Avenue, Vanderbilt, and the nearby Gulch. The menu focuses on great steaks, lamb, veal, and pork—it's meat heavy—and really good seafood. As you might expect from a Rayburn location, there's a remarkable wine list.

This is the place in Nashville where you really do want to start out with the #1 Ahi Tuna Tartare (and, yes, they aim for sustainable seafood), and follow it up with a beef tenderloin filet or a good veal preparation. If there's game on the menu on a given night, with Uhl as chef, take the risk and order it.

Midtown shines in a downtown where you'll find plenty of big chain steak houses, not just for its commitment to sourcing locally where possible and sustainable eating, but because the food truly is outstanding and keeps up with the high Rayburn standards.

I asked Midtown for a starter, and they provided this rich, fabulous smoked salmon option. I don't think you can go wrong trying to impress a dinner party with this one, and the addition of the touch of heat via the Tabasco makes it stand out.

SMOKED SALMON DRESSING
(SERVES 6)

8 ounces cream cheese

2 ounces anchovies

1 cup chopped garlic

2 cups heavy mayonnaise

2 tablespoons fresh lemon juice

1 tablespoon capers

1½ teaspoons Tabasco

¼ cup fresh dill

3 pounds smoked salmon, roughly chopped

Pull cream cheese from refrigerator and allow to soften.

Meanwhile, place anchovies and garlic in a food processor and process until coarsely chopped. Add mayonnaise, lemon juice, capers, and Tabasco, and process until anchovies and garlic are small flecks.

Add softened cream cheese and pulse until completely incorporated. Add chopped fresh dill and pulse until it is also completely incorporated.

Mix the salmon dressing with the chopped smoked salmon, and serve with toast points or crackers.

BEETS & HEAT SALAD

(SERVES 4-6)

2 pounds golden beets, diced

2 tablespoons extra-virgin olive oil,
   or more to taste

Salt to taste

1 pound fresh arugula

1 head fennel, julienned

2 oranges, segmented

Tabasco Honey Vinaigrette (recipe follows)

½ pound goat cheese/chèvre

½ pound candied pecans (recipe follows)

Preheat oven to 350°F.

Toss the diced beets in olive oil and salt to taste. Roast for about 45 minutes, until tender. Allow beets to cool to room temperature before the next step.

Thoroughly mix beets, arugula, fennel, and oranges with vinaigrette. When ready to serve, garnish with goat cheese and candied pecans.

CANDIED PECANS

½ pound whole pecans

2 egg whites

½ teaspoon salt

¼ cup sugar

½ teaspoon ground cumin

½ teaspoon cayenne

Preheat oven to 325°F.

Mix all the ingredients. Strain off the excess egg whites, then place the pecans on a nonstick silicon pad.

Roast for 12–15 minutes, then cool before using to garnish your salad.

TABASCO HONEY VINAIGRETTE

¼ cup Tabasco

½ cup clover honey (or honey to your liking)

½ cup vegetable oil

Mix all the ingredients together until thoroughly combined.

SHRIMP & GRITS
(SERVES 6)

Shrimp and grits in the South come in many forms. Once upon a time it was a Low Country specialty you only saw in Charleston or Savannah, but that moment has passed. Now most cities in the South have their own takes on the dish, and its popularity is spreading well beyond the borders of the traditional South, as residents of the North and the Midwest discover the humble grit.

For the grits:

½ quart chicken stock

½ quart heavy cream

2 teaspoons salt

Pinch of pepper

1 cup grits

¼ pound white cheddar

For the Tabasco butter:

1 pound butter, softened

¼ cup Tabasco

1 teaspoon honey

Pinch of salt

For the shrimp:

36 shrimp

1½ cups sliced red bell peppers

1½ cups sliced onions of your choice

Olive or canola oil for sautéing

To make the grits: Heat all the ingredients except the grits and cheese in a pan on the stove. Turn the heat to low, then add the grits.

Stir frequently until soft, about 30 minutes, then add the cheese.

To make the Tabasco butter: Mix all the ingredients together thoroughly, using a mixer.

To prepare the shrimp and assemble the dish:
Sauté the shrimp, bell peppers, and onions in oil until the shrimp is halfway cooked. Add the Tabasco butter and continue to cook until shrimp is done. It should be pinkish white and no longer translucent. Serve over the grits.

MISS DAISY'S CATERING

1110 Hillsboro Road, Franklin
(615) 599-5313
missdaisyking.com

Miss Daisy King epitomizes the Southern gracious lady, but behind her blazing smile and eloquent words there is the iron-willed talent that started the legendary Miss Daisy's Tea Room as a fearless twenty-something forty years ago, and who remains the grande dame of the Nashville food scene. She remains in constant demand as a caterer, speaker, and consultant, and her books continue to impact new generations of Tennessee cooks. Her take-out meals underline her fundamental style and high standard of taste (by more than one definition of that word). Grassland Market, where she set her business in the last edition, has closed, but the indefatiguable Miss Daisy continues on, catering and cooking for her myriad fans around the country, and her new location makes her even more convenient for those who want to drop in and order for catering or pick up something to go.

Miss Daisy is a reminder that the best and most quintessential Southern food is based on fresh, seasonal produce made with simplicity. Asked what exemplifies Tennessee cooking, she tells me: "Any Southern heirloom recipe, be it entree, cake, vegetable . . . While we've reached a new level in the South in the past ten or so years, it comes down to a few elements: fresh, simple, pure, but delicious food—true farm-to-table." And, she adds, that's what makes it appeal across the nation these days.

The three recipes that follow are utterly Southern—once

upon a time, every Southern homemaker had a cheese wafer/cheese straw recipe she put out for guests. Some of us are lucky enough to have family recipes, but if we don't, this is a fine standard to set now. Hot artichoke dip has had many incarnations at trendy fooderies across the nation since the '50s or '60s, but this is a very basic, simple variation you can make with good Parmesan and know your guests will love it. The black bean salad plays on the popularity of three-bean salads in twentieth century Southern entertaining, but adds a distinctly Southwestern touch. This is one of the dishes she regularly offers for takeout at Grassland Market, and it's irresistible, at least when I'm shopping.

PECAN CHEESE WAFERS

(MAKES ABOUT 75 WAFERS)

8 ounces sharp cheddar cheese

1 cup butter, softened

1½ cups self-rising flour

1 cup finely chopped pecans

⅛ teaspoon cayenne pepper

Grate the cheese, then let it soften with the butter in a bowl. Mix in the remaining ingredients.

Roll dough into logs about 1½ inches in diameter and place them on waxed paper. Chill for several hours.

Slice in thin wafers about ⅛-inch thick. Bake in a 350°F oven for about 8 minutes or until browned.

MISS DAISY'S HOT ARTICHOKE DIP

(SERVES 8 AS AN APPETIZER)

1 (14-ounce) can artichoke hearts, drained

½ cup mayonnaise, or more to taste

½ cup Parmesan cheese

⅛ teaspoon garlic powder, or more to taste

⅛ teaspoon paprika, for garnish

Preheat oven to 350°F.

In a bowl, mash artichokes well. Mix in mayonnaise, Parmesan cheese, and garlic powder.

Pour into a 1-quart ovenware glass dish and bake for 20 minutes or until bubbly.

Sprinkle with paprika to garnish.

Serve with your favorite crackers, melba toast rounds, or tortilla chips.

MISS DAISY'S BLACK BEAN SALAD

(SERVES 8, ¾ CUP EACH)

3 cups cooked black beans

1 red bell pepper, chopped

½ green bell pepper, chopped

⅓ medium red onion, chopped

2 green onions, sliced

1 rib celery, finely chopped

3 Italian plum tomatoes, seeded and chopped

1 cup cooked yellow corn

1 tablespoon olive oil

1 tablespoon chopped fresh cilantro

1 tablespoon fresh lime juice

1 tablespoon fresh lemon juice

½ teaspoon hot pepper sauce

½ teaspoon ground cumin

¼ teaspoon salt

¼ teaspoon black pepper

In a large bowl carefully combine the first eight ingredients. In a separate bowl, whisk together the remaining ingredients. Pour the dressing over the salad and toss thoroughly.

THE MOCKINGBIRD

12th Avenue North, Nashville
(615) 741-9900
themockingbirdnashville.com

The Mockingbird exudes whimsy when you walk in the door, replete with giant bird head sculpture on the wall. Beyond the Alice In Wonderland–esque décor is a menu full of marvelous delights, clean, straightforward, chef-driven.

Created by Brian Riggenbach and Mikey Corona, the executive chef and GM respectively, who arrived in Nashville via their friendship with the powerhouse that is Maneet Chauhan, the Mockingbird works toward being a fresh expression of the city's established locally sourced, fresh food ethos. Riggenbach and Corona have never before had a serious brick and mortar, but they masterminded a popular Chicago-based pop-up dinner club, Yo Soy. Chauhan remains a silent partner in The Mockingbird.

The menu showcases foods meant to be shared, with plenty of cross-cultural inspiration. Cross-cultural expression shouldn't surprise anyone since Chauhan arrived in town to become its epitome. Riggenbach and Corona build on that foundation, and we should look forward to more to come.

THE BIRD IS THE WORD

(SERVES 8)

For the gravy:

10 ounces Mexican chorizo

3 tablespoons all-purpose flour

3 tablespoons butter, at room temperature

1-quart milk

For the potatoes:

5 russet potatoes

1 stick butter

½ cup heavy cream

8 ounces salsa verde

Salt and pepper to taste

For the chicken:

1 quart buttermilk

Vinegar-based hot sauce

16 boneless skinless chicken thighs

Neutral oil for frying

2 cups all-purpose flour

3 eggs, lightly beaten

Salt and pepper

To prepare the chicken: Place the buttermilk in a large bowl, add as many dashes of hot sauce as fit your fancy (we like it hot). Place the chicken in the buttermilk and refrigerate at least 1 hour, up to overnight.

To make the gravy: Sauté the chorizo in a saucepan, cooking and stirring occasionally until cooked through, about 5 minutes.

Drain off any excess fat.

Combine the flour and butter, then mix the roux into the chorizo, and cook until golden, about 2 minutes,. Whisk in the milk and bring to gentle simmer.

Cook the gravy until thickened and slightly reduced, 8–10 minutes. Keep warm.

To make the potatoes: Boil the potatoes until soft, then remove to a stand mixer fitted with a paddle attachment, and let cool slightly. Add in the butter, cream, and salsa verde. Paddle the potatoes together until light and fluffy, about 6 minutes. Season with salt and pepper. Keep warm.

To make the chicken: Heat the oil in a large pot to 350°F. Remove the chicken from the marinade and set in a bowl. Then set up two bowls, one with flour and one with the eggs, season both with salt and pepper.

Dredge the chicken into the flour, then the eggs, then once again in the flour for good measure, shaking off any excess. Fry the chicken in batches until cooked through and golden brown, about 8 minutes per batch.

Once you remove the chicken, place on a wire rack, and tent with foil while the rest of the chicken is cooked.

To plate: Place the mashed potatoes on a plate, top with two pieces of chicken, then spoon the gravy over the top. Serve immediately.

MY VEGGIE CHEF

Delivery service
(Kitchen) 1500 2nd Avenue South, Nashville
(615) 200-8638
myveggiechef.com

Kristie and Matthew Holdren created My Veggie Chef to provide a vegetarian and vegan alternative to a very meat-heavy Nashville restaurant world—and local diet, and it's turned out brilliantly. If you don't believe me, check out the online reviews.

Matthew says: "We started it in August of 2011. It was Kristie's brainchild, really. She'd just graduated college with a degree in health, and had become fascinated with veganism and eating a vegan diet. We talked to a few of our friends and discovered that some of them were interested in a vegan diet as well. During these discussions, several of our friends told us that they'd be willing to pay us to make vegan meals for them. So, we saved up $500 to pay a month's rent on a commissary kitchen space, and made our first twenty meals (five each for four of our friends) during our first week.

"Before we knew it, we were making vegan meals for around twenty customers per week, and had to set up a delivery service to get all the meals to those customers in a timely manner. From that time up to now, we've hired a kit-building crew of three employees, a delivery crew of six drivers, and serve approximately one hundred twenty customers a week. That's a good deal of growth from the initial twenty back in 2011, and we're hoping to grow even more and continue to serve our meals for years to come."

The growth comes because the food is delicious, familiar, and wonderfully original. These white bean and turnip tacos are a great example.

WHITE BEAN AND TURNIP GREENS TACOS

2 cups cooked white beans

½ cup diced green peppers

½ cup diced onions

1 cup turnip greens

2 teaspoons vegetable base

½ teaspoon garlic powder

¾ cup water

Tortilla shells

Sour cream, if desired

Salsa, if desired

Heat a skillet over high heat. Mix ingredients in a bowl, pour into skillet, and cook on high for 10–15 minutes (or until water is evaporated and veggies are tender).

Stuff completed mixture into your choice of tortilla shells.

Add sour cream and salsa as desired.

PARTY FOWL

719 8th Avenue South, Nashville
(615) 624-8255
and
127 SE Broad Street, Murfreesboro
(615) 617-3909
partyfowl.com

Party Fowl is a Nashville hot chicken concept that's grown into a local favorite, adding a new location in Murfreesboro in late 2017, and a third in Donelson in 2018. The short version of the story is that owners Austin Smith and Nick Jacobson opened the restaurant with executive chef Bart Pickens with the aim of bringing terrific bar food into a spectacular bar setting. The specialty was hot chicken and cold drinks, The menu features chicken dishes with heat levels ranging from mild to "Poultrygeist," and chicken not hot at all—but still toothsome and delicious.

Did I mention local beers and craft cocktails? I moved to Murfreesboro recently, and Party Fowl is already redefining the city's cocktail culture, as it helped to do in midtown Nashville. Of course, it's also where you want to be for a Titans, Preds, or Vandy game—or maybe MTSU's Blue Raiders?

With that in mind, here's the perfect game-watching dip:

SMOKED CHICKEN DIP

2 cups mayo

2 cups cream cheese (softened)

2 pinches fresh chopped parsley, chopped

5 pounds smoked chicken, pulled (if you're making it yourself, try making a traditional beer can or beer butt chicken)

Salt

Pepper

In a large bowl, mix together mayo and cream cheese. Add the parsley. Fold in the pulled chicken. Add salt and pepper to taste and serve with chips.

THE PATTERSON HOUSE

1711 Division Street, Midtown
(615) 636-7724
thepattersonnashville.com

The dynamic Goldberg brothers, Ben and Max, have spent the past several years wonderfully putting their own stamp on Nashville dining. Their revival of old standby Merchants into something that's a well-frequented and innovative eatery made locals take notice, but it was the arrival of the Patterson House Speakeasy that truly set a standard for the city in terms of what we expected from our cocktail culture. (It doesn't hurt that they've opened their hit Catbird Seat upstairs, where the chefs serve up a splendid study in wholly original micro-gastronomy for a thrilled tiny few each night.)

The Patterson House is hidden away on the corner of Division Street in a big, purply-gray house that seems unobtrusive from the outside, but gives way upon entry to a stunning parlor-bar decorated in antiqued mirrors, vintage books, and elegant metallic wallpapers. It keeps that sense of retro 1920s going with its vast bar. Beyond the subtle glamour, the thing that you go for, aside from those little doughnuts that everyone always orders, are the cocktails.

Changing with the season, endlessly innovative, and daring us to step beyond the simple things we've had at every other bar we've ever been to, the Patterson House dares us to take a risk—and we never regret taking it.

DUCK HUNTER

"Sweet Lucy is a whiskey-based orange apricot liqueur—it's sweet and warming with rich fruit notes. Adding an egg yolk provides the drink with a beautiful richness. The allspice lends a nice spice note to the fruitiness, while the lemon adds freshness and acidity. The bitters enhance the orange in the drink," the folks at the Patterson House tell me.

1 egg yolk

2 ounces Prichard's Sweet Lucy Liqueur

¾ ounce fresh lemon juice

¼ ounce St. Elizabeth Allspice Dram

½ ounce simple syrup

9 drops 50/50 Bitters*

Crack the egg and separate the yolk into a shaker tin. Add all the liquid ingredients, including the bitters. Shake all the ingredients once without ice. Add ice and shake again, vigorously. Strain into a small glass with no ice or a coupe glass. Serve.

*Note: 50/50 Bitters are a blend of half Fee's Orange Bitters and half Reagan's Orange Bitters. Buy both Fee's and Reagan's bitters at amazon.com or your favorite specialty store.

PINEWOOD SOCIAL

33 Peabody Street, Nashville
(615) 751-8111
pinewoodsocial.com

I hate to use generation terms, but Pinewood Social represents the millennial ideal in ways few other Nashville venues have managed. It's a coffee shop, a place to nosh, and a place to work or network. Its also a place to bowl a few games on a reclaimed retro bowling alley or lounge in a mini pool in your trendy high-waisted bikini (replete with food served poolside from a vintage Airstream). And all of this is awesome, and appeals to those of us who count as Gen X or Gen Z as well, it turns out (I suspect our Boomer parents might even enjoy it). The "social" part of the title is completely valid—and this place is wonderful.

Chef Wil Uhlhorn has created a menu that varies with the time of day and playfully appeals to the mood of guests by the hour. Whether you want breakfast, lunch, dinner—or a midday snack, Pinewood has something right up your literal alley.

WHIPPED BLUE CHEESE TOAST

For the blue cheese mousse:

6 ounces heavy cream

10 ounces blue cheese at room temperature

6 ounces cream cheese at room temperature

¼ teaspoon salt

¼ teaspoon ground black pepper

For the completed dish:

2 ½" thick slices of sourdough bread

2 tablespoons unsalted butter, softened

2 JonaGold applesm cut in ½-inch slices

2 tablespoons local honey

4 tablespoons toasted walnuts

To make the blue cheese mousse: Whip the cream to soft peaks, then combine the rest in a food processor and puree till smooth. Fold all together.

To complete the dish: Heat a grill or cast-iron pan to medium heat. Brush the bread with the softened butter. Grill or toast the bread in the pan. Spoon the mousse over the toast.

Arrange the apples on the toast. Drizzle the honey and top with walnuts. Slice and eat warm.

PROVENCE BREADS & CAFE

Closed

I'll start this by saying that Provence is gone, closed in early 2018. That's a loss for the city, to say the least, but the memory will hopefully inspire a new generation of bakers. The baguette recipe is an astoundingly good one, so it needed to stay in this book for posterity. Provence had several locations throughout the city, and they served the community as our favorite *boulangerie*. Any number of the city's restaurants proudly offered up sandwiches on Provence's wonderful breads. But Provence itself was the kind of place you want to hang out at with friends, drinking deep cups of coffee or tea, eating sandwiches and pastries, and soaking in the atmosphere that is Hillsboro at its best.

Hillsboro Village sits at the confluence of Vanderbilt and Belmont University neighborhoods, just north of the busy Green Hills suburb. Somehow, though, the energy around it seems calmer, mellower. It's a collection of some of the city's best eateries and charming small boutiques. You can sit and people-watch from Provence's windows almost endlessly, catching sight of big-name stars and ordinary students. (One of the things you must love about Nashville is that stars are rarely harassed—no wonder they want to live here.)

Before I married, I used to sit here with friends constantly, I was running in and grabbing bread or cookies or handmade salads to go until the day it shut its doors. I mourn it.

Of course, you have to have a bread recipe from Provence, and they've given us a proper baguette. This recipe makes fourteen small loaves—so either plan on freezing some of them or divide it to a smaller proportion for more ready use. It produces a delicious, crusty bread perfect for serving with meals, dipping in oil and herbs, or eating by itself fresh from the oven.

FRENCH BAGUETTES
(MAKES 14 SMALL BAGUETTES)

For the poolish (your starter):

8 ounces bread flour

8 ounces water

Pinch of fresh yeast

For the baguettes:

1 pound poolish

1 pound plus 12 ounces bread flour

1 ounce salt

1 ounce fresh yeast

16 ounces water

Mix the poolish ingredients by hand until wet. Let sit in a covered bowl for 6 hours.

Mix the baguette ingredients by hand until a tight gluten structure forms, about 12 minutes. Let rest for 1 hour.

Divide into 14-ounce pieces and pre-shape rounds. Shape into baguette forms. Proof on board for 1 hour.

Score tops of loaves. Place in 500°F oven and bake for 30 minutes.

CREAMY TOMATO BASIL SOUP

(SERVES 8–10)

This is one of two takes on tomato soup in this book. You'll find the other in the Grilled Cheeserie entry (see page 106). Each one is delicious; this one relies on heavy cream and white wine, French-style, to give it heft and body, and it pairs really well with some fresh bread for dipping.

2 cups diced onions

¼ cup olive oil

½ cup white wine

¼ cup roasted garlic

12 cups San Marzano–style whole
stewed tomatoes

Salt to taste

2 cups water

1 cup heavy cream

½ cup roughly chopped fresh basil

Croutons and basil chiffonade, for garnish

Cook onions on medium-high in olive oil until lightly browned. Add wine, garlic, tomatoes, salt, and water and bring to a simmer. Turn heat down to low and let simmer gently for 45 minutes to 1 hour.

Add cream and basil and cook for 15 minutes.

Remove from heat and puree in a food processor for 3–5 minutes until smooth and fully blended.

Garnish with croutons and basil chiffonade to serve.

PUCKETT'S RESTAURANT & GROCERY

120 1st Avenue South, Franklin
(615) 794-5527
4142 Old Hillsboro Road, Leiper's Fork
(615) 794-1308
114 N Church Street, Murfreesboro
(629) 201-6916
500 Church Street, Downtown
(615) 770-2772
puckettsgrocery.com

Andy and Jan Marshall's Puckett's Grocery without a doubt qualifies as a local landmark in Leiper's Fork, perhaps even an icon, as you add together its multiple locations (including the new Puckett's Boathouse just at the outskirts of downtown Franklin, a location in southern Williamson County in Columbia; and the popular alternative food truck, Puckett's Trolley). In the beginning it was about good food and good music, and it still is today, whichever of their restaurants you choose to patronize. A quick perusal of the website will tell you who is playing at which locale and when.

Everyone across the city knows Puckett's, and the downtown Nashville location at Fifth and Church Streets, right next to several of the city's best art galleries, has raised the bar for the restaurant even more.

My most recent visit to Puckett's Franklin location, in the process of writing this book, involved my entire family, including my parents, my visiting aunt and uncle from Virginia, my uncle's sister, and my own sister and her two boys, ages one and five. Needless to say, we were a boisterous table, but it was the perfect place to relax over a long breakfast and have a great visit. Puckett's is a family place—you can bring the kids here and know they'll eat, and there's something for everyone on the menu.

Of course, in the evening when a band is playing, it's the kind of place you can bring a significant other or group of friends, and the atmosphere will be just as appropriate. The menu focuses on good, hearty food, whether you're coming in for eggs, bacon, and French toast at breakfast; a good sandwich for lunch; or a serious dinner that involves a Black Angus rib eye, chicken-fried steak, or the famous cherry-smoked baby back ribs.

PUCKETT'S CHICKEN SALAD

(SERVES 6–8)

Chicken salad is a thing here in the South, and Puckett's version is as traditional as they come, with pecans and fruit. You can feel equally good serving this one on a bed of lettuce to "ladies who lunch" or on some thick slabs of homemade bread to the guys who've been out working all day.

2 pounds chicken breast

1 cup grapes, cut in half

¼ cup pecan pieces

¼ cup diced celery

1 tablespoon sugar

1 teaspoon salt

1 teaspoon white pepper

1 teaspoon thyme

1 cup mayonnaise

Boil chicken breast until done (165°F). Shred the chicken and allow to cool.

Combine the chicken and the remaining ingredients in a mixing bowl. Mix thoroughly and allow to cool.

PUCKETT'S KING'S FRENCH TOAST
(SERVES 4)

When they say it's "King's" French toast, you get they mean Elvis, right? The Memphis-born rock-and-roller did plenty of recording here in town, back in the day, at RCA Studio B downtown. Those days are long gone, but we like to remember the great Mr. Presley by serving meals he would have loved—and we know he loved him some peanut butter and banana sandwiches. Puckett's tribute to that love is this wholly delicious French toast sandwich, perfect for brunch or breakfast. Don't even think about a calorie count.

4 eggs

1 cup heavy cream

1 teaspoon cinnamon

½ teaspoon nutmeg

½ cup peanut butter

8 slices sourdough or egg bread/challah

4 bananas

¼ cup butter

Powdered sugar, to sprinkle

Beat eggs in a mixing bowl. Whisk in heavy cream, cinnamon, and nutmeg.

Spread peanut butter across bread. Cut bananas in half and again lengthwise. Place bananas across 4 of the slices of bread, then top with the rest of the bread to make 4 sandwiches.

Dip entire sandwich into egg and heavy cream mixture.

Butter a griddle pan or skillet on medium heat. Place sandwich onto the buttered surface. Once the sandwich begins to crisp, flip. Brown both sides to desired crispness.

Cut sandwich in half and sprinkle with powdered sugar.

DRINK NASHVILLE

Not many years ago, the notion of Nashville native spirits and microbeers would have elicited a look of confusion on the faces of city residents. In less than a decade, that's all changed.

Part of that is due to changes in Tennessee law made under former governor Phil Bredesen in 2009, which now allow for microdistilleries within Tennessee city limits, with voter approval.

Franklin's Mike Williams, the mastermind behind Collier & McKeel Whiskey, had a lot to do with lobbying for that law change. Now the Speakeasy Spirits campus on 44th Avenue North, founded by Jeff and Jenny Pennington, produces Collier and McKeel, and Whisper Creek Tennessee Sipping Cream, Picker's Vodka, and Penningtons' Whiskey—among others.

Along with Williams for the law-changing ride were Darek Bell and Andrew Webber of Corsair Artisan Distilleries, who started out making their spirits in Bowling Green, just across the Kentucky state line, while the state legislature fought it out. (Now only their bourbon is made there; whiskey, gin, vanilla vodka, moonshine, and spiced rum all come from their distillery at Marathon Motor Works.) Corsair now also has one of the best microbreweries in the state, headed by the superbly gifted Karen Lassiter (women have beer power in Nashville) making some excellent stuff. They've recently opened a second distillery in the Wedgewood Houston neighborhood as well.

The Nelson Brothers upped Nashville's whiskey market by reviving Nelson's Greenbrier Distillery—the company started by their several times great grandfather, that prior to Prohibition rivaled Jack Daniels' and George Dickel.

Not too far down the road, find real (but legal) moonshine in Woodbury at Short Mountain Distillery, or venture to Thompson's Station in Williamson County for H.Clark. The big news is the recent purchase

of 55 acres in Murfreesboro for Sazerac's new distillery. And of course, Pritchard's has a small distillery space in North Nashville at the Fonatanel.

If we've gone spirit mad, we've developed an even greater beer culture. Yazoo Brewing Company products are now distributed all over the country, and a good bottle of Pale Ale or Dos Perros can be had by nearly anyone. The all-girl team at nearby Jackalope Brewery in The Gulch is producing some very fine beers as well. Blackstone Brewery is an eatery that's made a big name as a brewery and only keeps getting better. Maneet Chauhan's Mantra Artisan Ales has become a dominant force in Franklin, and her partners Derrick and Kayleigh Morse and Chad Frost are preparing to open a new campus in Murfreesboro.

East Nashville's Fat Bottom Brewery has taken off—that's a great neighborhood for beer—and exciting new places are coming along in Williamson and Rutherford Counties nearby. Murfreesboro's Mayday Brewery is deservedly gaining fans, with a fabulous location in an old factory and regular live music. Good local microbrewed beer is dominating even our chain restaurants these days—it's a real win.

Other local breweries are building up, too. Keep your eye out for Black Abbey, Turtle Anarchy, Tennessee Brew Works, Czann's, Bearded Iris, Southern Grist, Cool Springs Brewery, and Smith and Lentz Brewing.

RED PONY

408 Main Street, Franklin
(615) 595-7669
redponyrestaurant.com

Set in a century-old building off Franklin's downtown square, Red Pony has been the supreme monarch of fine dining in Franklin since Jason McConnell opened it in 2006. Williamson County in general, and Franklin in particular, has been a legendary chain restaurant haven, and McConnell's arrival on the scene did a great deal to help end that reality.

With its aged wood and brick, and soft red, gold, and brown color scheme, the whole restaurant is washed in warmth. From the moment you enter, no matter what it's like outside, the atmosphere soothes you, and it's easy to enjoy your meal, whether you're sitting at the bar watching ESPN or dining with a big group of friends.

I admit spending plenty of time at the bars (there's one upstairs, too), but I've also spent evenings here with friends, gathered around a larger table that still feels intimate. Chef Carl Schultheis pulls off plenty of impressive menu items himself—he and McConnell work brilliantly together.

Sitting at the bar, order from the starter menu—the tempura sushi roll is excellent and generally stays on the menu across seasons, as does the handmade guacamole and a terrific Tennessee tapas plate of local meats and cheeses—and I love the roasted Brussels sprouts as a light meal. When it comes to entrees, if you're partial to Middle Tennessee's take on shrimp and grits, Red Pony does a fine job, and the beef tenderloin is always delicious. For dessert, the pot de crème or the crème brûlée deserves serious consideration. And, of course, nightly specials increase the wonderful options.

BRAISED PORK SHANKS WITH RED WINE JUS

(SERVES 8)

8 pork shanks (around 1 pound each, on bone)

Salt and pepper to taste

½ cup flour

¼ cup olive oil

2 yellow onions, small diced

2 carrots, peeled and small diced

3 ribs celery, small diced

3 tablespoons chopped garlic

¼ cup tomato paste

1 bottle full-flavored red wine (whatever you like that is inexpensive)

2 sprigs fresh rosemary

2 sprigs fresh thyme

2 bay leaves

Water to cover shanks (meat only) in deep-sided casserole or dish of choice

Salt and black pepper to taste

2 tablespoons chopped Italian parsley, for garnish

Season the shanks generously with the salt and pepper, then dust with flour. Heat a large heavy bottom pan on the stovetop with the olive oil and brown shanks on all sides, working in batches if necessary.

Remove shanks. Add vegetables and garlic and sauté until golden brown. Then add the tomato paste and quickly stir into the vegetables. While continuing to stir, cook the tomato paste for about 5 minutes.

Deglaze pan with red wine, and add the herbs and bay leaves. Arrange shanks in your baking dish of choice, add the vegetable mixture and cover the meat with water. Cover the dish with a lid or foil.

Place in 350°F oven for 1½–2 hours, or until a skewer slides in and out of meat with ease.

Remove liquid from the dish and reduce on stove top to desired consistency. Season with additional salt and pepper if necessary, to taste.

Garnish with vegetables and reduced red wine jus, and finish with Italian parsley.

SINEMA

2600 8th Avenue South, Suite 102, Nashville
(615) 942-7746
sinemanashville.com

The wonderful old Melrose Theatre went through a plethora of incarnations before the coming of Sinema, but here's hoping this one lasts for a long, long time. Not only because of the historic location and the brilliant way the space has been repurposed, but also for the food, the ambiance—really the whole shebang.

The Melrose neighborhood features several great restaurants, including The Melrose, with its burgers and craft beer, and the nearby Yellow Porch—and It sits close to the rapidly growing old Wedgewood-Houston neighborhood with the new Corsair Distillery location—but the most elegant of the choices is Sinema.

Sinema offers a rich menu of classic American dishes, sometimes with Mediterranean accents and influences. This pasta dish from Chef Kyle Patterson is American-style Italian and pure comfort food. (It also teaches you to name your pasta ball.)

WHIPT RICOTTA AGNOLETTI
(SERVES 6-8)

For the pasta:

3 cups plus 2 cups fine white flour

14 egg yolks

1 whole egg

1 teaspoon Morton's Coarse Kosher salt

$\frac{1}{10}$ cup olive oil

For the ricotta:

2 quarts whole milk

1 pint plus 1 pint heavy whipping cream (used separately)

1 tablespoon (divided) Morton's Coarse Kosher salt, plus 1 pinch

$\frac{1}{8}$ cup champagne vinegar

$\frac{1}{2}$ ounce chopped garlic

$\frac{1}{2}$ teaspoon chopped fine herbs

Equipment

Cheese Cloth

Twine

Stand mixer, hand mixer or a whisk and elbow grease

Rolling pin (an empty wine bottle works in a pinch)

Pasta Machine

Piping bag

Brush

Wooden spoon

Knife or pasta cutter

For the Tomato Buerre Monte:

$\frac{1}{2}$ pint sundried tomatoes

1 pint heavy whipping cream

$\frac{1}{2}$ pound cold butter, cubed

Salt to taste

Shaved parmesan, to taste

Pinch black lava salt

To make the ricotta: Put the milk, 1 pint cream, and salt in a heavy-bottom sauce pot. Bring to a boil and immediately cut the heat, add the vinegar and let sit. The vinegar will force separation of the curd from the whey. Let it steep for approximately 30 minutes. Strain in a chinois lined with cheese cloth and catch all the curd. (You can save the whey and use it for various things such as soaking beans/grains). Once the curd is strained and in the cheese cloth, tie into a ball and hang in refrigeration for at least 6 hours.

To make the pasta ball: Pour flour in a circular mound onto a large, clean, smooth surface. Create a divot in the center of the flour. Add your egg yolks, whole egg, salt and olive oil into the divot. With a fork, begin mixing into the flour. Once you have a lumpy paste of a dough, being kneading the dough by hand until it becomes smooth, shiny and gives a good amount of spring back resistance. Name your pasta ball, per the chef, and let rest for at least 30 minutes.

Once these steps are complete, do the following:

Method for whipt ricotta: In mixer with a whisk attachment whip ricotta, remaining pint of cream, garlic, herbs and a pinch of salt on high until smooth and creamy. This is a great place to improvise, the chef's go-to is garlic and herbs but feel free to sub, swap, and play around with different fillings for your recipes. Transfer into a piping bag.

Method for rolling pasta: Once your ball has been named and is done napping, use a rolling pin and roll into an oval or oblong shape about a ½-inch thick. Make sure you liberally coat everything in flour.

Starting your pasta machine on setting 1, feed your pasta through. After it has been feed through at 1, fold your pasta over and onto it self and feed through on 1 again. Proceed setting 3 and feed it through again, fold again and drop it back down to 1 and run it through. Once the pasta sheet is squared off nicely with smooth edges feed it through on setting 3 and then 5.

For the agnolotti: Once the pasta has been rolled, the fun begins. Lay out your sheets of pasta, they should be about 5 inches (give or take depending on the size of your pasta machine) in width. Cut them in half, lengthwise and separate. Now that you have a long sheet of pasta about 2½ inches wide, brush the entire surface of the sheet with olive oil and pipe your whipt ricotta onto the edge of the pasta.

Roll your pasta tightly into itself leaving a ¼-inch lip on the end (this lip will catch the sauce).

Once you have a ricotta pasta "tube," take your wooden spoon handle and press down onto the tube at 2-inch intervals creating little pasta mounds. Once you've done this to the entire sheet, using a knife or pasta cutter, cut through the center of the divots and voila! Agnolotti.

Cooking the agnolotti: Drop pasta into boiling water; after about 4 minutes it will begin to float and it's done.

To make the tomato buerre monte: Add sundried tomatoes into heavy whipping cream, bring to a simmer and steep for 5 minutes. Blend until smooth. Blend cold cubed butter in, one piece at a time until fully emulsified. Salt to taste. Toss agnolotti in buerre monte and garnish with shaved parmesan and black lava salt.

THE SOUTHERN STEAK & OYSTER

150 3rd Avenue South, Downtown/SoBro
(615) 724-1762
thesouthernnashville.com

The Southern Steak & Oyster first made waves because it provided a truly good place to have a serious breakfast meeting over good food downtown. They manage far more than an excellent breakfast, fortunately, including lunch, dinner, Sunday brunch, and up until midnight on the weekend, if you happen to wander over from the grand, glorious Schermerhorn Symphony Center next door after a concert. That it happens to sit at the top of the Pinnacle Building, providing incredible city views as you dine, doesn't hurt either.

The Southern is part of the TomKats family, meaning they put a quarter century of highly successful catering and restaurant business knowledge behind this venture. They've put a lot of thought into what makes this place work—and while the focus, as the name suggests, is really steak and oysters (via a state-of-the-art, shuck-to-order oyster bar), there's plenty more on the menu to grab your attention.

The Southern strives to be many things—it's got both casual and fine-dining space and a comfortable bar where you can sit back and be yourself. What you find yourself appreciating is that it can successfully be many things at once and still define itself effectively, via a solid menu that emphasizes Southern foods with a little bit of twist—think of it as a branch of New American cuisine.

I really love this as a breakfast spot, I have to admit, but there's plenty to be said for drinks and oysters late on a summer afternoon, as my friend Dara Carson and I can attest.

BBQ SHRIMP

(SERVES 2 AS AN APPETIZER)

The Southern has seafood clearly in its sights—that's obvious. This is a marvelous alternative to a traditional shrimp cocktail and a terrific way to start off a meal.

3 tablespoons diced onion

1 teaspoon chopped garlic

1 tablespoon olive oil for cooking

5 large head-on shrimp

Salt and pepper to taste

2 tablespoons white wine

¼ cup BBQ Butter (recipe follows)

Chopped chives and grilled slices of French bread for garnish

Sauté onions and garlic in olive oil until soft, approximately 1 minute. Add shrimp and cook for another 3 minutes. Season with salt and pepper. Deglaze with white wine and reduce by half.

Add ¼ cup BBQ Butter and cook until butter is melted and shrimp are cooked.

Place shrimp and all of the pan's contents in a shallow bowl and garnish with chopped chives and grilled French bread.

BBQ BUTTER

(YIELD: ABOUT ½ CUP)

1 stick (½ cup) unsalted butter, room temperature

2¼ teaspoons lemon juice

¾ tablespoon minced shallot

½ tablespoon Cajun seasoning

½ tablespoon paprika

¾ teaspoon minced garlic

¾ tablespoon chopped parsley

¾ teaspoon Worcestershire sauce

¾ teaspoon salt

Mix butter in an electric mixer with a paddle attachment until smooth. Add all the remaining ingredients and mix until incorporated, scraping sides of bowl with a spatula to ensure seasoning is distributed evenly.

MY WAY (PASTA)

(SERVES 1)

Fans of spaghetti carbonara will love this tomato-free variation on eggs and pasta. With bacon lardons and goat cheese, you can easily serve this as a breakfast or brunch dish, but that doesn't preclude using it at dinner. I'm a big fan of pine nuts and cook with them every chance I get—they add a lovely nutty flavor to this dish that really seems to complete it.

2 tablespoons butter

1 teaspoon chopped garlic

2 ounces bacon lardons, cooked

5 ounces linguine, cooked

Salt and pepper, to taste

2 farm-fresh eggs

3 ounces goat cheese

2 tablespoons toasted pine nuts

1 tablespoon scallions, plus extra for garnish

Melt butter over medium heat and cook until milk solids begin to brown. Quickly add garlic and bacon lardons to pan and cook for 30 seconds.

Add linguine and season with salt and pepper. Continue to cook until hot.

Break egg and scramble throughout the pasta until egg is cooked.

Add goat cheese, pine nuts, and scallions. When cheese melts, plate the pasta.

Cook the remaining egg sunny-side up and place on top of the pasta. Garnish with chopped scallions.

WILD & LOCAL

Nashvillians love seafood, which is sometimes ironic given Tennessee's lack of a sea coast. We do have a fair amount of freshwater, and with that comes plenty of freshwater fish, but we covet those from saltier sources.

Fortunately, we're blessed with some great suppliers. I recently came across Wild & Local, one of the best of those, via their shop in the Nashville Farmers' Market. It astonished me that I hadn't realized the quiet men in the corner stall of the market house were fishmongers, but it was a fortuitous discovery.

Though most of the day's seafood was destined for restaurants (their clients include most of the establishments in this book, among them Flyte, Red Pony, Table 3, 1808 Grille, Saffire, Yellow Porch, Merchants, and City House), passersby can purchase the rest for themselves—which we do.

A company with a bold goal of sustainability, Wild & Local Foods sees their mission as an effort to encourage chefs and home cooks to understand exactly from whence their food came, and how it was caught and raised. They source fish from the fishermen and other meats locally from Tennessee farmers (they also deal in game meats, beef, pork, and poultry).

On my last visit, an ever-changing chalkboard above the shop front listed the food available and the market price. It's not cheap, but the quality is exceptional. On that day I bypassed the Louisiana redfish, the crawfish, and the halibut, but took home fresh diver scallops from Maine and oysters from the Gulf Coast. They were delicious, and for a Nashville home cook, not just a typical dinner.

Wild & Local is at 900 Rosa L. Parks Boulevard, inside the Nashville Farmers Market; wildand local foods.com.

SUNFLOWER BAKER

Baker Abby Stranathan came to Nashville via Louisville and Lexington, Kentucky, with an internship at the Biltmore under her belt and hopes of building a following for her sweets. A pastry chef at the Hilton Downtown's Trattoria Il Mulino, she also produces artisan cakes, cookies and baked goods for special occasions. (She made an incredible unicorn cake with glittery almond buttercream for my friend Lara's birthday, which is how I came to hire her to make almond cake for my mom's birthday.)

Stranathan learned her love of food from her grandmother, and it's a recipe from her grandmother she shares. Follow Abby on Instagram @sunflower_baker

GRANDMA'S APPLE CAKE

2 cups flour

1 teaspoon baking powder

½ teaspoon salt

1-2 teaspoons cinnamon

4 apples, small dice

4 eggs

2 cups sugar

½ cup melted butter

½ cup vegetable oil

1 teaspoon vanilla

Measure out flour, baking powder, salt, and cinnamon into a bowl. Put the apples in a separate bowl and toss them with a small scoop of the dry ingredients, just enough to coat them. Whisk eggs and sugar together until lemon-colored, and then add in the butter, oil, and vanilla. Stir in the dry ingredients and mix until they just come together. Fold in the apples.

Pour into a well-greased 8 x 8-inch square or 9-inch round pan. Bake at 350°F for 50-60 minutes.

SWAGRUHA

900 Rosa L. Parks Boulevard (Nashville Farmers Market), Germantown
(615) 736-7001
swagruhaindianrestaurant.com

I've been a big fan of Indian cuisine since I can't remember when, and Nashville's Indian restaurants are excellent. One of my absolute favorites is Swagruha, inside the Nashville Farmers Market. Owner Siva Pavuluri makes me feel utterly at home every time I go. When I was working from an office downtown, that was once a week—so I got to know her rather well. So well, in fact, she once brought me a gorgeous violet-and-green silk scarf back from a trip to India—which speaks to her generosity.

When you arrive at Swagruha for lunch, there's inevitably a line, with customers of every possible ethnic background, all looking for a very excellent meal.

There's nothing I've tried here that isn't delicious—I could, and have, make a meal out of the samosas—but really, Siva excels with her excellent butter chicken and chicken tikka masala. Fortunately, when you order from her counter, you can try both, and a bit of her equally fabulous vegetable korma, over a bed of fragrant vegetable rice.

For those looking to serve a vegetarian main course (not vegan, since there is yogurt involved), this is a wonderful meal all in itself. Rich and full of spices, it will make your kitchen smell like heaven and your guests very happy.

VEGETABLE KORMA

(SERVES 8-10)

5 medium-size potatoes

1 cup diced carrots

½ cup vegetable oil

½ teaspoon mustard seeds

½ teaspoon cumin seeds

2 cups sliced onions

3 teaspoons salt

1 teaspoon turmeric

1 cup green peas

1 tablespoon chili powder

1 teaspoon ginger garlic paste (available at international grocery stores)

2 medium-size tomatoes, diced

¼ cup grated coconut

2 cups yogurt

1½ teaspoons garam masala powder

1 tablespoon chopped coriander leaves (optional)

Cut potatoes into halves, then boil and peel. Cut the potatoes into ½-inch squares. Boil diced carrots.

Heat oil on medium-high for 2 minutes, then add mustard seeds. When the mustard seeds begin to pop, add cumin seeds. Add onions, salt, and turmeric and sauté until onions are clear. Add potatoes, carrots, and green peas.

Fry on medium heat for approximately 10 minutes. Then add chili powder, ginger garlic paste, and tomatoes and continue to fry on medium heat for an additional 5 minutes.

Add grated coconut, yogurt, and garam masala. Cook on low heat for approximately 10 minutes or until the oil rises to the top. Optionally, garnish with coriander leaves.

Serve with rice, naan, or roti.

Table 3 Restaurant & Market

3821 Green Hills Village Drive, Green Hills
(615) 739-6900
table3nashville.com

Wendy Burch and Elise Loehr had already proved their mettle with F. Scott's when they took on a challenge: French bistro/brasserie Table 3, complete with an adjacent patisserie—Table 3 Restaurant Market, so customers could not only come in for a good meal, but also take home a few sandwiches, cookies, or the take-out Blue Plate of the Day if they don't have time to linger.

It is perhaps unexpected that French country cuisine has not had a big following in Nashville until now. We've had our proliferation of Italian food, but it's only in the past few years that we've really come around to appreciate French as we ought. Table 3 brought French culinary sensibilities to the heart of Green Hills—arguably the busiest and most bustling shopping and business district in the city.

This is the place you can go if you want those fried frogs legs, frisée aux lardons, or crispy duck confit as starters, to be followed with cassoulet, rabbit fricassee, or coq au vin (I recommend it here). It's true French cookery, the way you want it done, with every aspect properly tended to. Table 3 stands out for the quality of its food, the breadth of its wine list, and an atmosphere reminiscent of true brasserie style.

I am thrilled to have the bouillabaisse recipe below—there's nothing that says true French cookery like it, and Table 3's is a hearty meal that reminds us why we wish we had more trips to the French coastlands planned.

BOUILLABAISSE
(SERVES 6–8)

½ cup olive oil

1 cup diced onion

1½ cups diced fennel

2 cloves garlic, minced

Zest of 1 orange

1 teaspoon saffron

½ teaspoon toasted and ground
    red pepper flakes

2 teaspoons salt

5 Roma tomatoes, diced

1½ tablespoons tomato paste

2 cups dry white wine

1½ tablespoons Pernod

Juice of 2 oranges

2 cups fish stock (recipe follows)

18 medium-size shrimp

1 pound halibut, cut into chucks

30 mussels, de-bearded and scrubbed

Salt and pepper

Rustic bread or baguette, sliced in
    long pieces and toasted

Rouille (recipe follows)

Table 3 Restaurant & Market   199

In a medium-size stock pot over medium heat, sauté in olive oil the onions, fennel, garlic, orange zest, saffron, and red pepper flakes. Season with salt and cook for 10 minutes. Add tomatoes, tomatoes paste, white wine, Pernod, orange juice, and fish stock. Simmer for 20 minutes.

Prior to cooking, season shrimp and halibut with salt and pepper. In a large pan over medium heat, sear halibut in olive oil until golden brown, 1–3 minutes. Add shrimp and mussels and ladle in broth to cover fish by two-thirds. Cover and simmer until mussels open and fish and shrimp are cooked, about 4 minutes.

Serve in individual bowls with equal portions of halibut, shrimp, and mussels in each; ladle in broth and cover fish by about one-third. Serve with the toasted bread slices smeared with Rouille.

FISH STOCK
(MAKES ABOUT 1 QUART)

2 tablespoons olive oil

1 yellow onion, diced

1 carrot, diced

1 leek, diced

4 pounds whitefish bones and shrimp shells

In a medium stock pot, heat olive oil over medium heat and add onions, carrots, leeks, and bones and shells. Add enough water to cover solids by 2 inches.

Simmer for 30 minutes, strain thoroughly, and discard solids.

ROUILLE
(MAKES ABOUT 1½ CUPS)

1 red bell pepper

1 jalapeño pepper

2 cloves garlic

1 cup aioli (see recipe below or purchase a high-quality mayonnaise)

Salt and pepper, to taste

Roast and peel the red bell pepper and the jalapeño.

Combine all the ingredients in a food processor and puree until smooth. Salt and pepper to taste.

AIOLI
(MAKES 2 CUPS)

2 large eggs

2 large egg yolks

2 cloves roasted garlic

1 clove raw garlic

2 cups canola oil

1 tablespoon plus 1 teaspoon fresh lemon juice

2 teaspoons kosher salt

½ teaspoon white pepper

Table 3 Restaurant & Market   **201**

Put the eggs, egg yolks, and roasted and raw garlic in a food processor and process to combine. While mixing, begin adding the oil slowly, blending until emulsified and thickened. Add the lemon juice, salt, and pepper. Keep refrigerated.

ONION SOUP GRATINÉE

(SERVES 6)

I think if you polled people and asked them to name a single French dish, the vast majority would respond with "French onion soup." I suspect there's a very good reason for that answer—it's flavorful and hearty, and there's absolutely nothing like it when on a cold, rainy day. The depth of this particular recipe allows for a myriad of flavors to balance out the onion, making it smooth and luscious.

1 bay leaf

3 sprigs thyme

2 cloves garlic

¼ cup black peppercorns

2 tablespoons butter

5 yellow onions, julienned or finely sliced

1 teaspoon salt

¾ cup sherry

1 cup brandy

3 cups veal stock

1 quart chicken stock

Salt and pepper to taste

1 baguette or white country bread, toasted and cut to fit individual bowls

6 slices Gruyère cheese

Additional items:

Cheesecloth

String

Oven-safe soup bowls

Make a sachet of the bay leaf, thyme, garlic, and black peppercorns by wrapping them in cheesecloth and tying off with string. Put aside.

Melt the butter in a medium-size sauce pot over medium heat. Add onions and salt, stirring frequently for 5 minutes, then reduce heat to low. Continue cooking, stirring as needed, until caramelized, about 30 minutes.

Raise heat to medium-high and add sherry and brandy. Reduce liquid by half.

Add veal stock and chicken stock and bring to a simmer. Add the sachet and simmer with the stock for about 45 minutes. Remove the sachet and season to taste with salt and pepper.

Preheat the broiler to high.

Ladle the soup into individual soup bowls. Float toasted baguette/bread slices, top with Gruyère, and broil until golden brown and bubbling, about 3 minutes.

TAILOR NASHVILLE

1300B 3rd Ave. N.
Nashville, TN
TailorNashville.com

When I started the second edition of this book, Chef Vivek Surti was still the power-house behind the VEA Supper Club, but we always knew he was destined for something like Tailor Nashville. Vivek isn't in this alone, he's partnered with talented Heather South-erland, who has had a tremendous success with the latest incarnation of local mainstay Frothy Monkey. The 2,000 square foot space in Germantown realizes the exuberance and originality of his more private meal efforts on a regular basis for patrons. The restaurant keeps the supper club/pop up concept feel too, with a prix fixe menu nightly. Vivek has a gift for potables, so expect the best cocktails as you walk in the door as well as old school levels of service from the staff. Reservations for the two sittings––one at 6, one at 8––are coveted, and can be made no more than a month out, so make sure you schedule your visit.

MUGHAL CHICKEN WITH RAITA AND BASMATI RICE
(SERVES 4-6)

1 whole chicken

½ cup neutral cooking oil

2 red onions, finely chopped

2 bay leaves

3 green cardamom pods, lightly crushed

2 star anise

2 cinnamon stick

3 cloves

6 garlic cloves, finely chopped

1 4-inch piece fresh ginger

2–4 Thai green chilies

1 can of whole, peeled tomatoes

1 tablespoon whole coriander seeds

1 tablespoon whole cumin seeds

½ tablespoon whole black pepper

1 teaspoon fennel seeds

1 teaspoon fenugreek seeds

½ tablespoon turmeric powder

2 teaspoons kashmiri chile powder (available at your favorite Indian grocer or on Amazon)

2 tablespoons mixed nuts (pistachio, cashew, almond, peanut), finely chopped

¼ cup water (optional)

2 tablespoons cilantro

3 tablespoons unsalted butter

1-2 limes, cut into quarters

Cut the chicken into 10 pieces with bone-in, remove skin, and season with salt. Let sit for 30 minutes to an hour.

Heat ½ cup of oil. Add bay leaf, cardamom, star anise, cinnamon, and cloves. Fry spices in oil until fragrant, about 1 minute. Add the onions, season with salt generously, and cook on medium to medium-high heat for 15–20 minutes until onions are deeply brown. Add ginger, garlic, and green chilies to your pot and cook additional 5–10 minutes.

Grind coriander seeds, cumin seeds, black pepper, fennel seeds and fenugreek seeds until a coarse powder. Add to the pot with turmeric and kashmiri chili powder and let spices cook in the oil. Once the spices are very fragrant and turn a shade or two darker, add whole peeled tomatoes. Break tomatoes up with a wooden spoon and scrape any fond in pan.

Add in the mixed nuts and cook entire mixture until oil starts to release from mixture.

Add chicken into mixture, turning until evenly coated in masala. If mixture looks dry, add ¼ cup of water. Turn heat to medium low, cover and braise for about one hour or until chicken is tender.

When finishing dish, add butter to sauce and let melt. Garnish with cilantro and squeeze of lime.

RADISH RAITA
(SERVES 4)

1 16 oz container of full fat yogurt

1 tablespoon black mustard seeds

4-6 fresh radishes

kosher salt, to taste

Grind black mustard seeds in a mortar and pestle until lightly broken. Add yogurt to a bowl, add mustard seeds and chopped radishes. Mix together. Season with salt and serve alongside curry.

BASMATI RICE
(SERVES 4)

2 cups long grain basmati rice

4 cups water

4 bay leaves

1 cinnamon stick

1 teaspoon cumin seeds

Wash the rice with several changes of water until water runs clear. Add a small amount of oil to a pan over medium-high heat and add the rice. Season with salt and stir rice until evenly coated in oil. Add bay leaves, cinnamon stick, and cumin seeds to rice. Add water to pot. Let rice come to a boil then cover pot and lower heat to low. Cook for 15 minutes until rice is done.

An array of other dishes at Tànsuǒ

TÀNSUŎ

121B 12th Avenue N, Nashville
(615) 782-6786

If you ever expect Maneet Chauhan to stop challenging the city's culinary status quo, I suggest you give it up. Tànsuŏ is the most recent iteration of her magical mind, together with her partners in the marvelously named Morph Hospitality group. The name means "to explore" in Cantonese, and this restaurant invites you on an odyssey through the kind of pop culture Chinese dining you might expect on the street or in small diner-style restaurants, food carts, and the like in Beijing. The executive chef, Chris Cheung, invites you to explore the kind of Chinese food you just don't tend to get in middle America, and it's astoundingly good. If you're looking for some sort of hoity-toity upscale Chinese, you kind of get the opposite—the things real people eat.

With that in mind, the offering from Tànsuŏ is an American Chinese classic—General Tso's chicken. My understanding is this dish was created for American audiences, and now it's a mainstay in every Chinese-American restaurant in the US. Fair enough, but Chauhan and Cheung make it a bit more Chinese for you to make at home—and something incredibly good.

GENERAL TSO'S CHICKEN

(SERVES 6, FAMILY-STYLE)

For the chicken brine:

1 gallon of water

⅔ cup sugar

1½ cup salt

To taste:

Ginger

Coriander seed

Cumin seed

Garlic

Cilantro root

Black pepper

For the chicken:

5 pounds boneless, skin on chicken thighs (large pieces)

4 ounces cornstarch

2 eggs

Neutral oil for frying

For the sauce:

3 pints water

1½ cups white sugar

3 cups white vinegar

2 teaspoons minced garlic

2 teaspoons minced ginger

1 cup thin soy sauce

½ cup double black soy sauce

½ cup oyster sauce

3 teaspoons fermented rice (available at Asian groceries)

To prepare the chicken brine: Crush all seeds slightly, heat them in a small amount of water and the return to the mix with all the other ingredients.

To prepare the chicken: Lay chicken with skin flap spread out. Cut ⅓ of the thigh, then cut the remaining piece in half. Roll up the chicken in the skin. The chicken will not stay rolled up, but it will retain its

Tànsuŏ **207**

shape better if it is rolled. Marinate drained chicken in brine mixture for at least two hours.

Mix cornstarch with eggs and a touch of water. Let sit for two minutes. Remove the chicken from the brine, let drain. Mix the egg mixture with the chicken, then deep fry at 310°F until the chicken is 150°F.

To serve: Heat sauce over a medium high stove burner until boiling. Stir the chicken into the sauce. Plate it. Garnish with sesame seeds.

Trattoria il Mulino

144 5th Avenue South, Nashville
Hilton Downtown Nashville
(615) 620-3700

I first familiarized myself with Trattoria il Mulino when a friend became a sous chef there, but like the rest of the Music City public, kept coming back because it was worth the trip. Oddly enough, Nashville doesn't necessarily have enough good, serious Italian food—so Trattoria was an excellent addition to the downtown food scene. It's modelled, of course, on New York City's original Il Mulino, but the staff led by Chef Thomas Cook has defined it as something truly their own, complete with some local sourcing and some distinct area influences (although don't go looking for it to be yet another New Southern restaurant in Italian costume—this is a real Italian menu). There's a pretty solid wine list to round out your dining experience, as recognized by the *Wine Spectator*, and do not skip dessert here.

PORCINI RAVIOLI IN A CHAMPAGNE TRUFFLE CRÈME

MAKES ABOUT 70 RAVIOLI (SERVES ABOUT 10)

For the dough:

1 pound durum flour

1 tablespoon salt

1½ tablespoons olive oil

½ teaspoon ground dry porcini mushrooms

6 extra-large eggs

For the filling:

1 ounce minced shallots

1 ounce olive oil

3 cups finely chopped mixed mushrooms

1 cup fresh porcini mushrooms

Pinch truffle salt

Pinch black pepper

1 cup grated parmesan cheese

4 ounces Boursin cheese

1 teaspoon chopped parsley

1 egg

1 cup panko bread crumbs

For the ravioli:

3 eggs for egg wash

For the sauce:

1 teaspoon white truffle oil

1 teaspoon chopped garlic

2 ounces black truffle paste (available at gourmet food stores)

1 (750-milliliter) bottle prosecco or champagne

1 quart heavy cream

1 cup grated parmesan

Salt and white pepper to taste

To prepare the dough: Place all ingredients in a 5-quart stand mixer with dough hook. Mix for 15 minutes on low speed. Wrap dough in plastic wrap and let rest for at least 30 minutes.

To prepare the filling: In a large skillet, sauté shallots in olive oil until translucent, then add mushrooms and continue cooking until all liquid is cooked out. Then season with salt and pepper. Add

grated parmesan cheese, Boursin cheese, and parsley; let cool to room temperature. Once cooled, add the egg and bread crumbs. Place into a piping bag.

To prepare the ravioli: Roll out pasta dough into very thin sheets and keep covered with a moist towel. Lay one sheet down over a ravioli mold. Then pipe a small dollop of the mushroom mixture into each ravioli filling hole. Brush the bottom pasta sheet with egg wash, then lay the next pasta sheet over the top and seal by rolling a rolling pin over the top. Invert formed raviolis onto a sheet pan lined with parchment paper and repeat until all of the filling is used up.

Raviolis can be made up to 3 days ahead of time kept in the refrigerator.

To prepare the sauce: In a sauce pot, saute garlic in truffle oil lightly, then add the champagne, and let reduce by half. Add truffle paste and heavy cream, and let reduce again by half. Add parmesan, and season with salt and pepper.

To serve: In a large stock pot, bring water to a boil with a pinch of salt in the water. Add a few raviolis at a time into the boiling water for 3 minutes or until they float, then drain and toss into the truffle cream sauce. Place seven ravioli on each plate with an even amount of truffle cream sauce. Garnish with fresh shaved truffles. Bellissimo!

VUI'S KITCHEN

2832 Bransford Avenue, Nashville
(615) 241-8847
And
1120 4th Avenue North #101, Nashville
(615) 610-3383
Vuiskitchen.com

A Music City take on traditional Vietnamese, Vui's Kitchen underlines the fact that ethnic cuisine is taking off in Nashville at long last. Vietnam native Vui Hunt was raised in a large family for whom cooking and family always took priority. She brought those notions with her to the US, and her restaurant reflects the warmth of the kitchens of her youth. The food is comforting, flavorful and made with love, she says. She and husband John Hunt know how to make guests welcome and keep us coming back—a pretty solid beer and wine (and sake) list doesn't hurt, either.

The original Berry Hill location has now been joined by a Germantown space as well (in the spot once taken by Cochon Butcher). It's the perfect place to get really good Pho in town, as well as popular Vietnamese staple dishes such as Banh Mi (original, beef, and vegetarian). The salads are my personal favorites (try the Shrimp and Lotus Root when you're in), and this recipe provides a terrific way to bring rich, layered, slightly spicy Vietnamese tradition to your kitchen.

CABBAGE CHICKEN SALAD (*GOI GA BAP CAI*)

A blend of two distinct dressings gives this salad its robust, delicious flavor. Dressings and salad can be stored in a glass containers in the refrigerator for several days. A great time saver is to purchase a rotisserie chicken at the market and use it for the salad. It also tastes great without chicken or substitute pan-fried tofu cut into thin strips. You can sub gluten-free soy sauce in place of fish sauce.

MAKES 4 CUPS

For the salad:

3 cup shredded savoy cabbage, paper thin

1 cup sliced red onion, paper thin

1 cup julienned carrots

3 tablespoons chopped cilantro

3 tablespoons chopped mint

2 handfuls arugula

2 room temp/cool-poached chicken breasts

¼ cup toasted crushed peanuts (optional), sub other nuts if needed.

Tear chicken into thin strips with a fork. Combine all ingredients in salad bowl and set aside.

Note: Poach chicken in lemongrass and ginger for extra flavors.

For dressing 1:

½ jalapeño, sliced

¼ cup chopped cilantro

1 teaspoon garlic

1¼ teaspoon kosher salt

1¼ teaspoon black pepper

3 tablespoons honey

½ cup lime juice

½ cup olive oil

Place all ingredients except olive oil in a blender and blend well on medium setting. Switch to a lower setting and pour all olive oil in slowly until well mixed and emulsified.

For dressing 2:

¾ cup sugar

1 teaspoon garlic

⅛ cup chili garlic sauce

4 tablespoon fish sauce

¼ cup lime juice

⅛ cup warm water

Blend all ingredients in a blender on medium to high speed until well mixed.

To Finish: Combine both dressings together and mix with the salad as needed.

WHISKEY KITCHEN

118 12th Avenue South, the Gulch
(615) 254-3029
whiskeykitchen.com

Entrepreneur Chris Hyndman developed his M Street concept by making use of an entire city block downtown in the old, revitalized railroad gulch. After a local favorite, Radius 10, closed several years ago, he worked to turn that location and its mostly industrial block running along McGavock Street at the corner of 12th Avenue South into a concept collection of remarkably different restaurants. These included trendy Asian-fusion Virago, high-end steak house Kayne Prime, and a private members-only club. Right at the corner of the two streets, he turned a former Mexican restaurant into Whiskey Kitchen—and we loved it.

Boasting a plethora of really enjoyable menu items that play on the notion of Southern comfort foods, including some of the best sweet potato fries and sliders in town, Whiskey Kitchen also boasts a really amazing bar—and a solid tasting list of whiskeys, for those so inclined. The cocktails are plentiful as well, and very creative.

During the day you'll find plenty of folks taking a business lunch here or meeting for drinks after dinner. The outside pergola provides a welcome respite from the bustle of nearby Broadway. I spent a lot of time sitting here with coworkers in my magazine days, and plenty of late nights after concerts at nearby 12th and Porter with my music and fashion friends as well.

The recipe provided here is another take on the quintessential Tennessee favorite, macaroni and cheese. This is a little on the grown-up side, with a hint of heat to it. Definitely perfect to serve for your friends at a football party or the like and have them begging for more.

CHIPOTLE MAC & CHEESE

(SERVES 4)

8 ounces pasta shells or elbow macaroni

¼ cup unsalted butter

3 tablespoons flour

3 cups half-and-half

2 cups shredded white cheddar

½ cup white or yellow American cheese

1 teaspoon onion powder

1 teaspoon garlic powder

Salt and pepper, to taste

1–3 tablespoons chipotle peppers in adobo, minced or pureed

½ cup buttered bread crumbs, optional

Cook pasta of choice to al dente.

Melt butter over medium heat. Add flour and stir to make a roux.

Slowly add half-and-half to pot with roux, stirring until smooth. Continue to stir until sauce begins to thicken.

Add cheeses a little at a time, stirring constantly until smooth, then add spices, salt, pepper, and chipotle peppers. Add pasta and stir to combine.

The mac and cheese can be served at this point or placed in a baking dish, topped with buttered bread crumbs, and baked at 350°F for 30 minutes.

Whiskey Kitchen 215

THE YELLOW PORCH

734 Thompson Lane, Berry Hill
(615) 386-0260
theyellowporch.com

I've spent plenty of time on the porch that gives this cozy Berry Hill location its name, enjoying the herb and flower garden that somehow thrives a few feet from the busy stretch of Thompson Lane. Gep and Katie Nelson's Yellow Porch always seems, like its Brentwood sister Wild Iris, to have distinctly fresh (in all senses of the word) and creative takes on food.

Berry Hill has long been divided by Thompson Lane—there's the big Vanderbilt Health Center to the south that's taken over the old 100 Oaks Mall and revitalized it, and a host of innovative small businesses operating out of tiny '40s and '50s ranch-style homes to the north. The Yellow Porch sits right on the dividing line, serving the patrons of both worlds and all those who drive in as well.

The Yellow Porch gets extra credit for managing paella very well, and the sweet tea–cured smoked pork chop is marvelous. The lunch menu brims with excellent salads, including a very good take on the now-classic Black and Blue Salad, with seared sirloin, blue cheese, tomatoes, crispy onions, and herb ranch dressing, garnished with bacon and cucumber.

The recipe provided here for the cheese fritters is absolutely delicious. It's a perfect starter or appetizer to pass at a party. Chef Guerry McComas makes use of local favorite Sweetwater Valley cheddar cheese, which you can order from the website listed below, or substitute your own favorite sharp cheddar. These recipes are designed to be served together—the chow chow makes a wonderful, spicy contrast to the cheese fritters—and the fritters themselves dip right into the spicy, Sriracha-laced aioli.

TENNESSEE SHARP CHEDDAR CHEESE FRITTERS

(MAKES 16-18 FRITTERS)

1½ pounds Sweetwater Valley cheddar,* shredded

3 cups all-purpose flour

2 teaspoons baking powder

2 cups buttermilk

5 eggs

1 tablespoon Old Bay seasoning

1 tablespoon salt

¼ cup chives, chopped

Place all the ingredients in a stand mixer bowl and mix with the paddle attachment until well combined.

Using a 2-ounce scoop or 2 large spoons, scoop out and fry the batter at 350°F for 4–5 minutes or until each fritter is golden brown.

*Note: You can order Tennessee's Sweetwater Valley cheddar at sweetwatervalley.com, or substitute Cabot (Vermont) sharp white cheddar, available at most grocery stores. Any good locally made sharp white would also be excellent if available, according to Chef Guerry.

CHOW CHOW

(MAKES 2 QUARTS)

1 head green cabbage, shredded

1 yellow onion, small dice

1 red bell pepper, small dice

¼ cup kosher salt

1 quart cider vinegar

2 cups sugar

1 tablespoon dry mustard

1½ teaspoons turmeric

1 teaspoon ground ginger

1 tablespoon mustard seeds

1 teaspoon crushed red pepper

In a bowl, combine the cabbage, onions, bell peppers, and salt. Toss well and let sit for 24 hours.

Combine the vinegar and spices in a sauce pot, bring to a boil, and simmer for 10 minutes.

While the vinegar mixture is coming to a boil, drain the cabbage mix in a colander. Add the cabbage to the vinegar, bring back to a boil, and simmer for 10 more minutes.

Pour the mixture into a container, cover, label, and date. The chow chow can be used as soon as it cools down, however, the flavor will improve over time. It will keep for a month or more in the refrigerator.

SPICY AIOLI

(MAKES 1¼ CUPS, ENOUGH FOR THE FRITTER RECIPE)

1 cup mayonnaise

2 tablespoons Sriracha hot sauce

2 tablespoons Thai sweet chili sauce

Mix all the ingredients together and set aside to serve with the fritters. The aioli can be used right away, or it should keep for at least a couple of weeks in a sealed container in the refrigerator.

Plate the dish with aioli in the middle for dipping the cheese fritters and chow chow to garnish.

ART AND CULTURE

Nashville and Middle Tennessee have their own arts culture, including craft traditions from locals, immigrants, slave tradition, and colonial tradition, dating back centuries. The Tennessee Arts Council makes sure our original and traditional crafts are always on the radar. I have the good fortune to contribute to Nashville Arts magazine regularly, and get to follow our artisan culture. If you're in Middle Tennessee, here are a few festivals you may want to visit. Whether you want to celebrate a Victorian Christmas in Franklin or buy beautiful local creations in Cannon County, there's something here for everyone who wants to explore Middle Tennessee's artist community for the first time—or find a new hidden gem after years of living here.

Many of these festivals have years of tradition behind them, some dating back thirty, forty, or fifty, years. The arts and crafts celebrated may be well older.

March

Elk Valley Crafters Spring Craft Show, Fayetteville. Arts and Crafts show, only handmade crafts. Always the second Saturday in March. festivalnet.com/10315/Fayetteville-Tennessee/Craft-Shows/Elk-Valley-Crafters-Spring-CraftShow

Lewisburg Spring Craft Fair, Handmade crafts. Always the second Saturday in March. fcpccraftfairs.com/

Irish Day Parade and Arts and Crafts Festival, Erin. houstoncochamber.com/community-events/irishday

April

Art on the West Side. Nashville event featuring more than 50 artists in a variety of media including painting, glass, clay, jewelry, photography, wood, and fiber. nashvillejcc.org/adults/art-on the-west-side/

Slawburger Festival. Fayetteville, "We have such a rich history with the unique 'slawburger' and we want the festival to serve as a way to share those stories. Create new memories or revisit those memories from the past. Some events could include slawburger eating contest, Mr. & Miss Slawburger, a KidZone, and much, much more!" slawburgerfestival.com

The Nashville Cherry Blossom Festival. Family-friendly celebration of spring and Japanese culture. nashvillecherryblossomfestival.org

May

Spring Tennessee Craft Fair, Nashville. Join the Nashville tradition of celebrating and supporting American handmade crafts. Shop one-of-a-kind, finely crafted artwork directly from the juried, award-winning artists. tennesseecraft.org/events/craft-fairs

Tennessee Renaissance Festival, Arrington. Multi-weekend affair is set across 68 acres and features strolling musicians, magicians, more than sixty master artisans, a life-size castle, jousting tournaments, camel rides and theatrical performances. tnrenfest.com

Middle Tennessee Strawberry Festival, Portland. A new queen is named every year, with a beauty contest, carnival, golf tournament, 5-K run, and food and craft vendors as mainstays of the celebration; but the annual parade is still the center attraction! And Portland is a strawberry capitol for a reason. So delicious! cityofportlandtn.gov/strawberry-festival

June

The RC-Moon Pie Festival, Bell Buckle. Held annually on the third Saturday in June. This wacky, fun-for-the-whole-family event celebrates the South's original fast food—an ice cold RC Cola and a fresh Moon Pie. Smiling visitors from all over the world (we can prove it cause there's a "who travelled the furtherest contest!") stream into the downtown area where they find plenty of music, cloggers, weird and knee-slapping-fun contests, Moon Pie games, a colorful parade, and 5K run (burn off the peanut butter Moon Pies!). bellbucklechamber.com/bell-buckle-rc-moonpie-festival-general-info

Bonnaroo Music and Arts Festival, Manchester. So we're too young to have gone to Woodstock. We have Bonnatoo. bonnaroo.com

July

Uncle Dave Macon Days, Murfreesboro. There's nothing else like this: An annual old-time and Americana music festival that celebrates Uncle Dave Macon, legendary banjo picker, songwriter, and unique performer who became the first star of the Barn Dance, then Grand Ole Opry on WSM radio. It's a nationally renowned music competition and old-time clogging, buck, and free-style dance competition, a three-day event that brings over 40,000 old-time/Americana music and dance fans to Middle Tennessee. Craft vendors and demonstrations are on site. uncledavemacondays.com

August

Tomato Art Fest, East Nashville. Complete with a parade, wild art entries, merchants with special deals, and more. This is a wholly distinct local festival for adults and kids alike. There are twenty different activities and contests, vendors, drinks, live music, art, and all-around good times. tomatoartfest.com

September

White Oak Crafts Fair, Cannon County. The festival, in beautiful rural Cannon County southeast of Nashville and Murfreesboro, offers something of interest for everybody who delights in items individually designed and hand crafted. Demonstrators are on site as well. artscenterofcc.com/whiteoakcraftsfair.html

Clarksville's Riverfest, Clarksville. You'll enjoy art, music, family activities, and more all set along the Cumberland River. Take in a tour of

continued . . .

Beechhaven Winery while you're there. cityof clarksville.com/index.aspx?page=327

Fall Tennessee Craft Fair, Nashville. Join the Nashville tradition of celebrating and supporting American handmade crafts at this event. Shop one-of-a-kind, finely crafted artwork directly from the juried, award-winning artists. While shopping, you'll meet the artists, learn what inspires them and how they take raw materials and transform them into fine craft. tennessee craft.org/events/craft-fairs/

Upper Cumberland Quilt Festival, Algood. View more than 175 quilts and wall hangings made by local artisans, all entered for competition. Come see 800–1,000 quilts, quilted items, and needlework, plus art pieces on display at locations around the city. All vendors will be located where quilts are displayed, many demonstrating quilting techniques at their booths. Purchase jewelry, quilting supplies, crafts, and a wide variety of things vendors have for sale. quiltfestival.com

Grinders Switch Music and Arts Festival, Centerville. Arts, crafts, and more, plus several solid local wineries are nearby to add to your day out. hickmancountychamber.org/localevents/grinders-switch-music-arts-festival

Standing Stone State Park Marbles Festival and National Rolley Hole Championships, Hilham. The National Rolley Hole Marbles Championship and Festival finds the world's best marble players taking center stage in an event deemed the world's most challenging marble tournament. The event has been featured by a variety of national news channels and magazines. Live music, kids' games, marble vendors, tournament play, demonstrations, food, and marble fun for kids round out this fall event. tnvacation.com/events/hilham-35thannual-standing-stone-marbles-festival-national-rolley-hole-championships

African Street Festival, Nashville. The festival features arts and crafts, dance, drumming, storytelling, an eclectic mix of music, and more. aacanashville.org

Rock Island Lions Club Fall Festival and Craft Fair, Rock Island, Tennessee. The festival includes live music, food vendors, and craft vendors located at the natural sand beach. Plus explore this glorious state park (the author's parents have a house nearby, and I'm probably wandering the crowd). Grab dinner nearby at the Foglight Foodhouse. facebook.com/events/207921936000127

Indian Education Pow Wow and Fall Festival. Nashville. Features Native American dancing, music, food, arts, and crafts. naiatn.org/powwow

Fall Fest at the Hermitage, Hermitage. Features more than ninety artists showcasing paintings, jewelry, photography, basketry, ceramics, leather and more. Enjoy the spectacular weekend of art, music, and history at Andrew Jackson's Hermitage. fallfestatthehermitage.com

October

Artober, Nashville. A month-long celebration of the arts in Music City. Artober Nashville celebrations include hundreds of events in visual and performing arts, music, theatre, dance, craft, film, and more. visitmusiccity.com/Visitors/events/artober

Nashville Oktoberfest Fall Festival, Nashville/East Nashville. Features German and specialty food from dozens of restaurants and vendors, tons of kids and family events, world-class beer from local and German breweries, arts and crafts vendors, three stages of live German music, an enormous parade through downtown, Wiener Dog races, and the second largest 5K race and run in Tennessee—and so much more. thenashvilleoktoberfest.com

Autumn in the Country Arts and Crafts Fair, Centerville. Handmade and hand-crafted items sold. hickmanartsandcraftsguild.org/events/event/autumn-in-the-country-arts-crafts-fair

Clarksville Vintage Fair, Clarksville. Explore handmade, homemade, and vintage treasures at the Beachhaven Winery. clarksvillevintage fair.com/#shoppers

Nashville Cultural Festival, Nashville. Features a variety of dance and music performances, food vendors offering authentic and exotic tastes from around the world, hands-on children's activities, an area just for teens, a marketplace, and much more. More than sixty music and dance performances on five different stages. Vendors sell and demonstrate their hand-crafted items. celebratenashville.org/world-market

Celebration of Nations, Franklin. Features music on two stages, beer tasting, and multiple craft and food vendors. Throughout the day the stage will feature music and dance from around the globe. sistercitiestn.org/programs/events

National Banana Pudding Festival, Centerville. In addition to the National Cook-Off for the Best Banana Pudding in America, there's also the Puddin' Path where you can sample banana puddin' made by ten local nonprofit organizations. There will be food for everyone, many varieties of banana pudding to try, and more. bananapuddingfest.org

Tennessee Craft Week (second week in October), Nashville and other locations. A series of happenings across the state. tennesseecraft.org/tennessee-craft-week

Off the Beaten Path Studio Tour, DeKalb and Cannon Counties. The studio tour includes more than thirty artists and multiple stops. offthebeatenpathtour.com

Webb School Arts and Crafts Festival, Bell Buckle. More than one hundred juried artists showcase their work in fields of pottery, fiber, jewelry, wood, baskets, paintings, sculptures, ironworks, photography, chainsaw carvings, botanicals, and more. Many of the artists give live, on-site demonstrations of their skills. Third weekend of the month. bellbucklechamber.com/webb-school-art-craft-show-general-info

Pumpkinfest, Franklin. The festival stretches along Main Street, and its avenues, and offers tons of festive fun for families. Street festival food and beer garden, the Great Pumpkin, extreme pumpkin carving, and more than one hundred artists and crafts people with hand-made wares line Main Street from First to Fifth Avenues. historicfranklin.com/events/event/pumpkin-fest

El Dia de los Muertos, Cheekwood Estate and Gardens. Nashville. This brings the traditions of Mexico and Latin America to Nashville with traditional music and dance, vibrant art activities, and authentic cuisine. Visitors learn about the culture of their Latin American neighbors while exploring beautiful altar displays and shopping in the marketplace. cheekwood.org/calendar/el-dia-de-losmuertos

November

The Goats, Music and More Festival, Lewisburg. Features musical entertainment, goat shows, goats gallop 5k, three-legged goat triathlon, food of every description, arts and crafts, and more. goatsmusicandmore.com/festival-info

Christmas Village Art and Craft Event, Nashville. Features more than 200 merchants from all over the US. A variety of outstanding seasonal and gift items are available, including toys for all ages, clothing for children and adults, jewelry, food items, pottery, and collectibles. christmasvillage.org

December

Dickens of a Christmas Street Festival, Franklin. I haul my pretty 1850s walking suit from the closet for this one. The festival features nearly 200 musicians, dancers, and characters who fill the streets. Come see and interact with the nefarious Fagin from *Oliver Twist*; Ebenezer Scrooge, Jacob Marley, and Tiny Tim from *A Christmas Carol*. And, of course, a Victorian Father and Mother Christmas with treats for children. Coming dressed in Victorian costume adds to the ambiance. There will be live artisan demonstrations plus more than one hundred vendors offering holiday arts and crafts on Main Street from Second to Fifth Avenues. historicfranklin.com/events/event/dickens-of-a-christmas

Resource Guide

Where to order all those fabulous regional food products

Arnold Myint
Smoked salt and other artisan products
arnoldmyint.com

Arrington Vineyards
Locally produced wines from Williamson County, favorites include Red Fox Red, Stag's White
6211 Patton Rd.
Arrington, TN 37014
(615) 395-0102
arringtonvineyards.com

Bang Candy Company
Artisan marshmallows, candies, and sweets, plus simple syrups for cocktails and baking
1300 Clinton St., Suite 127
Nashville, TN 37203
(615) 953-1065
bangcandycompany.com

Benton's Smoky Mountain Country Hams
Bacon, country ham, and pork products
2603 Hwy. 411 North
Madisonville, TN 37354-6356
(423) 442-5003
bentonscountryhams2.com

Bongo Java Coffee
Wholesale and retail fair trade coffees
2007 Belmont Blvd.
Nashville, TN 37212
(615) 385-5282
bongojava.com

Dozen Bakery
Cakes, pies, cookies, and more; made to order with organic ingredients
(615) 509-9680
dozen-nashville.com

Firepot Chai
Hand-blended chai concentrate from fair trade or better ingredients, custom teas
2905 12th Ave. S., Suite 106
Nashville, TN 37204
firepot.com

Goo Goo Clusters/Standard Candy Company
Tennessee original candies, wholesale and retail
715 Massman Dr.
Nashville, TN 37210
googoo.com

Kenny's Farmhouse Cheese
Artisan cheeses from the region, from Asiago to Swiss, plus gift baskets
2033 Thomerson Park Rd.
Austin, KY 42123
(888) 571-4029
kennysfarmhousecheese.com

Noble Springs Dairy
Goat's milk cheeses and other products
3144 Blazer Rd.
Franklin, TN 37064
(615) 481-9546
noble-springs.com

Olive & Sinclair Chocolates
Bean to bar handmade chocolate, in a variety of flavors
1404 McGavock Pike
Nashville, TN 37216
(615) 262-3007
oliveandsinclair.com

Roast, Inc. (8th & Roast)

Better than fair trade hand-roasted coffees
2108A 8th Ave. South
Nashville, TN 37204
(615) 730-8074
8thandroast.com

Silke's Old World Breads

Fresh, European-style, handmade breads, cakes, and pastries
1214 College St.
Clarksville, TN 37040
silkesoldworldbreads.com

Sunburst Trout Farms

Fresh trout, caviar, and other food products
128 Raceway Place
Canton, NC 28716
(828) 648-3010
sunbursttroutfarms.com

Sweetwater Valley Farm

A wide variety of cheeses, including flavored cheddars and cheese curds; farm tours welcome
17988 W. Lee Hwy.
Philadelphia, TN 37846
(865) 458-9192
(877) 862-4332
sweetwatervalley.com

Triple L Ranch

Free range meats, including beef
5121 Bedford Creek Rd.
Franklin, TN 37064
(615) 799-2823
lllranch.com

TruBee Honey

Regional Tennessee raw honeys and honey straws
trubeehoney.com

Whisper Creek Tennessee Sipping Cream

Original cream liquor made in Nashville, distillery tours available
900 44th Ave. North (SPEAKeasy Spirits campus)
Nashville, TN 37209
tennesseesippingcream.com; buy online at binny's
.com

LOCAL SPIRITS

Local Spirits in the book are available nationally through distributors. State laws make it difficult to buy some directly over the Internet. For more information please visit the following sites for products recommended in this book by Nashville mixologists.

Collier & McKeel Tennessee Whiskey
collierandmckeel.com

Corsair Artisan Distillery
corsairartisan.com

George Dickel Tennessee Whiskey
dickel.com

Jack Daniel's Tennessee Whiskey
jackdaniels.com

Nelson's Greenbrier Distillery (Belle Meade Bourbon)
greenbrierdistillery.com

Prichard's Distillery
prichardsdistillery.com

Short Mountain Distillery (Tennessee traditional moonshine)
shortmountaindistillery.com

Woodford Reserve Kentucky Bourbon
woodfordreserve.com

INDEX

ABOUT THE AUTHOR

Stephanie Stewart-Howard is a journalist, costumer, and artist, happily tech writing for a multi-national gaming company. Formerly an editor with Gannett, she's the author of three titles with Globe Pequot and numerous articles on art, fashion, travel, and nerd culture for publications including *Nashville Arts*, Livability.com, *Faerie* magazine, *Nashville Lifestyles, The Mary Sue,* and *Where Nashville,* among others. Stephanie was born in Virginia and brought up worldwide thanks to her dad's career in the US Air Force and corporate America. She lives with her tech professional husband Seth and two witty and intrepid felines in a contemporary Craftsman cottage just outside Nashville, where they cultivate a wild English garden and sip whiskey on the porch. The couple is active in the medieval and ancient world living-history movements, as well as a variety of arts and crafts.

photo by Stephanie May Saujon

ABOUT THE PHOTOGRAPHER

Ron Manville is a culinary/lifestyle photographer who has photographed dozens of cookbooks that have garnered national and international awards, including four James Beards. He is a contributing photographer for *Art Culinare, Grace Ormonde's Wedding Style* magazine, *Local Palate, Nashville Lifestyles,* and many other publications. Ron was Team USA's photographer at two IKA Culinary Olympics competitions in Erfurt, Germany, to highlight a long-term association with the American Culinary Federation. He is an RIT graduate and US Navy veteran, and he resides in Nashville.

PHOTO CREDITS

Most photos by Ron Manville with the following exceptions: pp. ii, iii f11photo/Shutterstock.com; pp. 12-13 Courtesy of Barlines; p. 28 Courtesy of Bob's Steak and Chop House; pp. 30, 32 Courtesy of Burger Up; pp. 46, 48 Courtesy of Carter's; p. 49 StelsONe/Shutterstock.com; pp. 50, 51, 53 Courtesy of Chauhan Ale & Masala House; p. 54 Courtesy of Chef's Market Café & Takeaway; p. 56 Courtesy of City House; pp. 58, 60 Courtesy of City Winery; p. 62 StockEU/Shutterstock.com; pp. 110, 111 courtesy of Hugh Baby's; p. 115 marekuliasz/Shutterstock; pp. 116, p. 119 Courtesy of Kitchen Notes; p. 121 Jim Davis/Courtesy of the City of Murfreesboro; p. 131 Aquir/Shutterstock.com; pp. 166, 167 Courtesy of The Mockingbird; p. 168 Brent Hofacker/Shutterstock.com; pp. 170, 171 Courtesy of Party Fowl; pp. 107, 108, 109 Courtesy of Sinema; p. 194 Evgeny Karandaev/Shuttertock.com; p. 200 Pixavril/Shutterstock.com; p. 204 Courtesy of Chef Vivek Surti/Tailor Nashville; pp. 206, 208 Courtesy of Tànsuŏ; pp. 210, 211 Lisa Diederich Photography/Courtesy of Trattoria il Mulino; p. 213 Marina Onokhina/Shutterstock.com; p. 220 SAHAS2015/Shutterstock.com.